A Beautiful Heritage

EMBRACING ABUNDANT LIFE

LAURA HINCHMAN

"Scripture quotations taken from the (NASB®) New American Standard Bible®, Copyright © 1960, 1971, 1977, 1995 by The Lockman Foundation. Used by permission. All rights reserved. www.lockman.org"

This book is memoir. It reflects the author's current recollections of her experiences over many years. Some names have been changed, some events have been compressed, and some dialogue has been recreated to convey the essence of the conversation. Stories often take on a life of their own. May this one honor the Life-giver of us all.

ISBN 979-8-218-14359-6

Cover designed by Hannah Linder at Hannah Linder Designs

Formatted by Catherine Posey at Hannah Linder Designs

Edited by Katie Williams at Storyborn Creative

Visit the author's website at www.laurahinchman.com

Contents

Dedication

*Brad, the love of my life. Thank you for saying
"yes" to this wonderful adventure.*

*Philip, Isaac, Abigail, Ruth, Samuel, Josiah, Simeon, Lydia,
Hannah, Elizabeth, Esther, and Ezra. Thank you for making me a
mom. I love you and I am so proud of each one of you.*

*Leah, Adrianna, Jamie, Emily, Sarah, Sylvia, and Asher (listed in
the order of joining our family). Thank you for letting me claim you
as my own. I never realized how much I would love you.*

Dad and Mom, you always believed I could do this.

Prologue: Foundations

~~~

The lines have fallen to me in pleasant places;
indeed, my heritage is beautiful to me.
Psalm 16:6

"I don't mean to alarm you, but I can't hear the baby's heartbeat."

The doctor stood beside me, pressing the fetal doppler a few inches below my belly button. My husband, Brad, stood on my other side, concern etched across his furrowed brows. I was in the first trimester of my first pregnancy. The doctor's words quickened my breathing into short, shallow gasps, but his movements remained calm and unruffled. I took my cue from him, inhaled deeply, and pushed away the threatening panic.

"It isn't unusual at this stage," the doctor was quick to reassure us, "but I want to send you down the hall for a quick peek, just to be certain."

The ultrasound room was small and dark. The technician applied clear gel to my still-flat belly and circled slowly with the hand-held transducer, pausing occasionally to squint at the screen or tap a key on the computer. Brad and I kept our eyes locked on the monitor, but all we could make out were shadows. The black and white images seemed indistinct to our unpracticed eyes, and I felt the panic swelling within me again. I licked my lips and glanced at Brad, wondering if he felt as confused as I did.

Finally, the technician pointed to a small spot on the screen. "Do you see this area that appears to be blinking?" She asked in a cheerful voice. "That's your baby's heartbeat."

Nothing else on the screen made sense to us, but we could easily make out the reassuring flicker. I vacillated between relief and wonder as I saw with my own eyes the evidence of God's handiwork pulsing inside my body.

Life—fragile and exquisite, mysterious and magnificent. From the youngest embryo to the oldest senior citizen, we are created and designed by our Lord for His eternal plan and glory.

Over and over in Scripture, we see the value and beauty of human life. Genesis 1:26-27 tells us of our birthright—of the wonderful privilege of being created in the very image of God. Psalms 139 reminds us that to be human is to hold inherent meaning and purpose since we are carefully and wonderfully knit together (see verses 13–14) for God's good pleasure.

What showed up on that ultrasound screen, with a merrily blinking heart, was nothing less than an invaluable, eternal soul. And I was his mother. The awe of that washed over me, as I held hands with Brad in that still, holy moment.

By this time in my life, I was already convinced of the preciousness of life and the value of motherhood. I had even volunteered for a short stint at a crisis pregnancy center early in our marriage. I believed that protecting little ones in the womb, encouraging women in difficult pregnancy situations, and speaking truth about the miracle of being created in the image of God were all sincere and good affirmations of the value of life. But they were only a beginning. As Brad and I prepared to embark on the journey of parenthood, God began to deepen our understanding of what it means to embrace life. In the years to come, He would stretch us with opportunities to live out that expanding comprehension in practical, beautiful ways.

As we would eventually learn, there is far more to embracing life than simply advocating for the unborn. In addition to honoring the life God creates in the womb, we also have the opportunity to steward our own lives in a worthwhile and meaningful way. Not only has God granted that we would have physical existence, but Jesus also came to offer us an abundant journey on this earth. John 10:10 states it clearly: "I came that they may have life, and have it abundantly." Jesus invites us into a full, vital adventure—walking with Him and experiencing the joy, peace, and intimacy He offers.

This is the foundation of a beautiful heritage—embracing life with Jesus.

In the broadest sense, we, as believers in Jesus, have a beautiful heritage rooted in eternal security. We are brought into God's family and are co-heirs with Christ in God's kingdom. No matter the situation of our lives here on earth, we have the guarantee of future glory that far surpasses any difficulty we encounter now (see 2 Corinthians 4:17). Our inheritance is imperishable and free of sin and every other hindrance attached to humanity since the fall. We can look forward to Eden again— joyfully and freely communing with God and enjoying His bounty.

But this beautiful heritage has implications for us here on earth as well as for eternity. God created us to journey with Him through this life and on the deepest soul level we long for that connection. *He* is life. *He* is joy. The Psalmist recognized this when he wrote, "You will make known to me the path of life; in Your presence is fullness of joy; in Your right hand there are pleasures forever" (Psalm 16:11). God offers a rich inheritance of abundance here and now—living a life *with* Jesus and *for* His glory.

As we walk with the Lord, we play a part in building our

beautiful heritage too. We can live our lives in a way that touches others and passes on a significant legacy of loving relationships and vibrant faith. We can leave an example of following hard after Jesus and loving Him wholeheartedly, inviting those around us to pursue their own wondrous adventure with God.

This book is about embracing life—honoring life as God creates it and living in the fullness that Jesus offers. For Brad and me, these two aspects—welcoming life and learning to lean into abundance—were intertwined so deeply that they were indistinguishable from each other. As the Lord stretched us into stronger, life-affirming actions, He also led us into greater, abundant-life adventure.

That day, as we gazed at the monitor, Brad and I didn't know that in the years to come, we would visit similar ultrasound rooms again and again. What at first appeared indistinct and unknowable, would eventually become recognizable and familiar, from the shadowy shapes and beating hearts of our babies to the strengthening presence and gracious heart of our God. The Lord would use those ultrasound screens to refine and transform us and to reveal the extent of the work He was accomplishing in our lives. They would become a tool to disclose some of His most precious gifts—the delightful as well as the difficult. Sometimes the machine would uncover deep sorrow, and we would acknowledge anew that God is not only the originator of life, but the One Who decrees the number of our days (see Psalm 139:16). The abundant life Jesus offers is not free of pain. Entrusting ourselves to Him, even when sorrow and struggle were our appointed companions, gave us the assurance of His peace and provision, and the comfort of His presence and love.

God has blessed us with twelve children, and now we are enjoying the gift of a new generation as we welcome our grandchildren. We've been surprised on many occasions as the Lord determined the "lines" of our narrative (Psalm 16:6), yet woven through the specifics of our particular drama is the common thread of God's goodness and faithfulness. His gracious character and leading can be stitched firmly within your narrative, too. Whether you have a dozen daughters, a single son, or no children at all, whether you achieve your dreams or find yourself in the most unexpected place imaginable, the path to a beautiful heritage is the same—embracing life, embracing abundance, embracing Jesus.

He is our beautiful heritage!

Good Beginnings

EMBRACING THE BEAUTY OF GROWING IN GRACE

But grow in the grace and knowledge
of our Lord and Savior Jesus Christ.
2 Peter 3:18

I've been a mother for as long as I can remember. Granted, my early ministrations tended to be a bit haphazard, but I still delighted in my maternal role and lavished much love on my baby dolls. The yellow-haired, blue-eyed Baby Tender Love dolls were my favorite. Emily could "drink" from a bottle and wet her diaper. Mary's rubber arms and legs moved. Lisa couldn't manage any of these magical feats but she still held a special place in my heart because she had been my first. I spent countless hours holding and comforting my "babies," changing their clothes, wrapping them in the soft swaddling blanket Mom had given me, and even occasionally scolding them when they were naughty.

One late afternoon, as I attended to my "girls," my imagination moved beyond the moment to embrace a future possibility. What would it be like to have a real baby? I paused and smiled at the thought, then stood abruptly leaving Emily, Mary, and Lisa to their own devices, as I ran to the kitchen in search of an answer.

"Mama, where do babies come from?" I gushed as I skipped up to my mother, shoe untied, and hair escaping from my ponytail. Tugging on the bottom of her shirt, I waited anxiously for the answer. I may have been fuzzy on the specifics at that age, but there was one thing I knew for sure—I wanted a baby when I grew up.

Mom paused in her supper preparations, turning from the stovetop to reply. She leaned over and smiled at me. "One day when you get married, if you love your husband very, very much, God will give you a baby."

"Oh, okay." I scooted away, taking her answer at face value, but filing it away to examine later.

And examine it, I did. "One day when you get married, *if* you love your husband very, very much, God will give you a baby." I latched onto that "if" and worked it to the best of my six-year-old ability. Since having a baby depended upon how well I loved my husband, I decided I'd better start convincing God of my sincerity—right away. So, I began pleading: *God, when I get married, I promise I will love my husband very much. Please, please, please give me a baby when I grow up.*

I was desperate to persuade the "Giver of Babies" that I needed to be a mom. Even at my young age, I was already attempting to manipulate the situation (and the Lord) to ensure everything turned out the way I thought it should.

And sure enough, seventeen years later, I married my college sweetheart and was beyond smitten. My desire for children had not diminished in the least but had solidified into a strong sense of purpose. There was not a specific encounter or event that I could claim as the reason for my persistent longing. I simply believed God had planted the desire to be a mother deep into my heart and was nurturing that yearning as a key component of the calling He had designed for me.

By the time I married, I knew two things: I wanted children and I wanted to stay home with them. Through the years I had given various answers and imagined various scenarios when asked what I wanted to do when I grew up, but what I always came back to—what I wanted more than anything else—was to be a mother.

Brad wanted children too, but we embraced the culturally acceptable attitude of waiting a couple of years before trying to conceive. It didn't occur to us even once to question that decision. It was 1988. That was how it was done, so that's what we did.

A little over a year into our marriage, some out-of-town friends visited us with their newborn. When they arrived, we exchanged greetings and hugs while my eyes drank in their son nestled securely in his car seat. I pulled him from his seat and held him close, cheek pressed against the top of his fuzzy head, ears tuned to the music of his soft grunts, nose heady with his sweet baby smell. My eyes locked with Brad's across the room, and a silent question passed like an undercurrent between us. Why were we waiting? What was so significant about the two-year mark before attempting pregnancy?

SHAPED BY CULTURE

The voices surrounding us are loud. We are shaped and influenced in subtle and not-so-subtle ways. The current opinions, the prevailing wisdom, and the prevalent theories are so much a part of our background that we accept them as truth without a second thought. They feel normal, even if they aren't right.

Mercifully, God sometimes jolts us out of our cultural stupor. I experienced one such intervention during my college years. One early spring day, lazy with sunshine, a friend and I were walking together after class, deep in a discussion about current events. Erin was someone I trusted and whose knowledge of and walk with the Lord I respected. The topic of abortion came up as we meandered through the center of our small campus. I had never thought seriously about the issue but, instead, let my opinion be formed by the conversation I heard in the culture around me.

When Erin asked my opinion on the matter, I turned to admire a budding dogwood tree before spouting the worldly wisdom I had absorbed. "I personally wouldn't have an abortion," I said, "but I think it's a woman's right to choose."

Erin raised her eyebrows. (Perhaps she wondered how I could appreciate spring's rebirth reflected in the beauty of nature all around us, but fail to fathom the infinite value of life in the womb—the irony certainly seems clear to me now.) Whatever Erin was thinking at that moment, she stopped walking and turned to face me before gently but unapologetically stating, "That's not right."

Now it was my turn to raise my eyebrows, astonished by her confident, bold divergence from the common cultural standard. "What do you mean?" I asked.

Erin sat on a nearby bench and patted the space beside her. I plopped down, curious to hear where this was going.

Erin began by quoting Psalm 139:13: "For you formed my inward parts; You wove me in my mother's womb." Then she looked up for a moment, apparently searching for what to say next. "I don't remember exactly how it's worded," she admitted, "but Jeremiah chapter one talks about how God had specific plans for Jeremiah before he was born." Erin propped her hands on her knees and leaned forward. "In other words, God created us and had plans for us while we were still in our mothers' wombs. We were just as human and just as loved by God before we were born as after."

My cheeks burned as I nodded. I knew she was right. I had been quick to accept the cultural perspective without considering what God might have said on the issue, and I had been easily duped by a lie and my own shallow reasoning.

That conversation was a crucial turning point for me and the beginning of my pro-life journey. I grieved that, even as a believer,

I hadn't ever thought biblically about the issue. I hadn't even thought through it logically. Looking back, the God-given value of human life should have been obvious, especially in light of my lifelong desire to be a mother. And yet in my ignorance, I had devalued the preciousness of a child's life because I was shaped more by the culture around me than by study and understanding of God's Word.

I'm not even sure where or how I had absorbed the abortion messaging. The news? Neighbors? The women's "right to choose" motto would not have been commonly embraced in my social circles, but because I had no grounding, I took it at face value whenever and however it appeared. I had attended church regularly in high school, but I had never heard a sermon or partic-ipated in a study addressing what Scripture had to say about abortion or any other social issue. As Erin and I talked that day, I realized that it was time for me to dig into the Word to figure out what God said. I wanted to strengthen what I believed and be able to articulate and defend it.

God used Erin to nudge me away from deception and into truth. In the same way, He used our friends' visit with their newborn son to confront Brad and me as a couple—prodding us to grapple with why we had so readily patterned our child-bearing choices after the other newlyweds around us. We had not made our decision based on truth or reason or even desire, and we had not asked the Lord what He wanted for or from us. We had simply followed typical cultural boundaries.

It wasn't only the unbelieving community encouraging us to wait. Even in our Christian circles, protocol prohibited the conception of a baby too soon in a marriage. Couples didn't just go on their honeymoon and return home pregnant. That was irre-sponsible. They went on the pill and waited a couple of years before jumping aboard the baby train. Without a thought, we waited right along with them.

ASSUMPTIONS TURNED UPSIDE DOWN

We had emulated those cultural patterns with no real thought about what we wanted, or more importantly, what God wanted. But seeing that sweet little boy turned our assumption on its head and jarred us out of our cultural fog. Why were we unquestionably conforming to a general societal expectation with no real consideration or evaluation in our specific marriage? And what was God's heart on the matter?

After our friends visited with their sweet baby, we began the conversation with each other and with God. We wanted to move forward with expanding our family but had some reservations. Was this the best time? How were we supposed to know? Would we somehow be jeopardizing our future if we didn't get the answers to these questions right?

I also had to face my childhood fear that I wouldn't be able to conceive—that my dream of being a mother would not be realized. Motherhood felt like a personal calling from God, but maybe I was mistaken. By then, I had realized that God didn't base the bestowment of children on my love for my husband, but I knew the Lord was the Giver of life, and I anxiously wondered if He would bless us with a baby.

After much prayer and agonizing, I went off the birth control pill. At first, the timing of my cycles seemed a little erratic as my body adjusted back to life without hormonal interference. But after a couple of months of unpracticed tracking, I thought I should be due for a period, and I purchased a pregnancy test. According to the packaging, I was supposed to be able to confirm that I was expecting by the intensity of the color of the liquid in a tiny test tube. However, all I could confirm was that I was confused. (Most of the home pregnancy tests in 1990 were not as dependable and easy to read as they are today.)

Frustrated and impatient with not having a clear answer, I drove to the local health department, hopeful that their tests would prove more reliable. When the test registered negative, I resigned myself to wait for another month, continuing to fervently pray that God would grant my lifelong desire for a child.

Another week crept by while I continued to implore the Lord and nurse my insecurities, but I still didn't start my period. Hope began to bubble up again and this time I didn't bother with the home pregnancy test or the health department. I had been volunteering at the local crisis pregnancy center, so I made a special trip to the low, red brick building and asked permission to use one of their tests.

A sweet older lady manned the desk and chatted with me while we waited together for the result. I stood across from her, straining to stay engaged and maintain eye contact while she spoke, but the pending pregnancy test swallowed my attention like quicksand. When she paused, I stole a glance and then blinked away the wetness pooling in my eyes.

"It doesn't look very good, does it?" I tried hard to keep the tremor out of my voice, but my shoulders slumped in disappointment.

"Sometimes these things take a little time," the volunteer said kindly. She smiled and nodded her head toward the test lying on the countertop between us.

I gasped as I took in what she had already seen—a faint but distinguishable line was now evident. My hand shook as I lifted the device for a closer look.

She laughed out loud, her silver hair bouncing gently. "Let me be the first to congratulate you!"

This time I didn't attempt to conceal my tears as I grinned at her, at the positive test, and back at her again.

My car somehow made its way home that day, though I don't remember the drive. I was focused on the miracle taking place in my body. *There's a **baby** in me! There's a baby in **me**! Oh, thank you, thank you, God!* Over and over the words danced through my brain as I tried to absorb the wonder: I am a mother.

We began spreading the news immediately to friends and family and almost anyone who would listen. Occasionally even strangers heard my fairy-tale announcement. My newly-pregnant status made me feel like a queen and I bore that title regally for the first couple of weeks...until the sickness began.

FALSE EXPECTATIONS

I'm a little embarrassed to admit it, but I honestly thought nausea was for women who didn't really want to be pregnant— for those who weren't "all in" on this baby thing. Of course, *I* wouldn't be sick. I'd dreamed of this moment for as long as I could remember. But the fairy tale was quickly becoming something other than what I had imagined.

I put a roast in the slow cooker one morning, noting that the meat smelled a bit strong. I didn't think much about it as I added potatoes and carrots with a liberal dose of onion seasoning. As the meal slowly simmered all day, so did my queasiness. Did I have a little bug?

The next day brought more of the same. Then the queasiness turned into full-blown nausea. With vomiting. For weeks.

And, of course, not just in the morning.

This wasn't exactly my dream come true. Instead of an idyllic and serene transition into motherhood, I was regularly hugging the toilet. Not a pretty picture nor a pretty reality. Thinking I wouldn't experience pregnancy sickness solely based on my level of excitement over the baby had been a naive assumption on my part. The nausea provided a quick adjustment of my unrealistic inexperience. Already, motherhood was proving to be more challenging than I had imagined.

Eventually, my sickness subsided, and I was able to enjoy my expectant state. God had granted what I so fervently desired. I was thrilled about my new role, but also nervous about what it would require of me. So far, I had allowed myself to be constrained by cultural norms and had harbored unrealistic expectations about pregnancy. And I was just getting started. What else would I discover?

PEOPLE-PLEASING AND PERFECTIONISM

Growing up, I was the good girl who tried hard to please everyone—God, my parents, my teachers, and any other adult who had influence in my life. People-pleasing was my penchant and early reinforcement strengthened that inclination.

I attended a small private school for kindergarten. One rainy fall day, all twenty-three of us remained inside for a loud but dry recess. During the week while services were not being held, we occupied a makeshift classroom and two smaller adjoining rooms in the church-turned-school building. We played with blocks and puzzles, trucks and books. On this particular day, my classmate, Amy—a petite, brown-eyed, dark-haired girl—and I wanted the same thing at the same time.

We tussled for a moment, both clutching the same yellow yarn-haired doll, subjecting its less-than-secure limbs to a tug-of-war. "It's my turn," I insisted.

"No, mine!" Amy argued with an extra yank.

The impasse might have lasted until the doll lost a leg, but Amy suddenly let go. "You take a turn first and then I'll play with her."

I looked into clear eyes that a moment before had been determined and unyielding. She smiled tentatively then reached for a couple of stray Lincoln Logs on the worn carpet beside her.

I clutched the doll and sat back confused, trying to take in her sudden about-face. She wasn't being manipulative or sneaky; it was a sincere offer. It only took two seconds before I wished I had been the one to make it. Somehow, I knew she had "won." Hers was the better response.

I watched Amy occasionally after that day and noticed several similar scenarios with other classmates. It's not that she didn't want to be first. The initial struggle proved that she did. But she battled herself more than her opponent, eventually winning the victory and usually a new friend, too. It was impossible to dislike her.

Several months later the whole class wiggled in line, waiting to march to the lunchroom when our teacher announced that she needed a bride for our upcoming kindergarten graduation program, *The Wedding of the Flowers*. Every girl in the room raised her hand, hoping, hopping, and pleading with her eyes. Not one of us was surprised, however when Mrs. Curtis walked over to Amy. She would be the bride and all of us knew she deserved it.

Amy's kindness and generosity were genuine, and deep down, I knew I wanted to be that kind of person, too. However, I also couldn't help but notice the side benefits: her kindness won her friends, gained the praise of adults, and put her in first place for a lovely surprise. My motives were mixed, but my mind was made up. I already tended toward people-pleasing, and Amy's example reinforced my resolve. I would be the good girl who did the right thing, not only because it was the right thing, but also because the right thing seemed to be the avenue to get good things in return.

PERFECTIONISM LEADS TO FEAR

Even as a child, my people-pleasing expanded into a perfectionistic, fear-driven mindset. I tied my security and significance to how well I performed, and I struggled with the fear of not measuring up. Because being the "good girl" was my identity, I was convinced that dire consequences would follow any less-than-stellar outcome. I didn't know exactly what those consequences would be, but I was sure I couldn't afford to find out.

Ballet lessons illustrated my dilemma. Miss Linda was graceful and beautiful, and I wanted to be just like her. She moved across the dance floor with a poise I couldn't hope to emulate.

"Now try this, girls. One, two, three, plié." The mirrored wall perfectly replicated Miss Linda's flowing movements.

I bit my lip as I attempted to emulate her, moving woodenly then stumbling over the unfamiliar steps and catching myself. I looked up quickly to see if she had noticed.

Miss Linda smiled encouragingly but my heart still thumped with fear. I had never seen her act harshly toward a student, but what would happen when I messed up one too many times? Would she snap? What would be the painful consequence? I feared finding out, so I told my mom I wanted to quit the lessons. My little-girl dream of being a beautiful ballerina was eclipsed by my dismay at what would happen when I finally triggered Miss Linda's displeasure.

I felt the same way about the Lord as I did my ballet teacher. Naturally, God was nice and He even loved me. After all, He was obligated. But I was sure there was a point beyond His patience, and I didn't want to find out what life was like on that side of the line. My only choice was to learn to maneuver very carefully. I couldn't let myself fail.

Of course, I did fail—sometimes with simple mistakes and other times by outright sin, but I always tried to make sure it wasn't too obvious. And I often tiptoed around God, feeling like I had a target taped on my back labeled, "Aim here in case of mess-ups."

I would like to think that I had shed some of my perfectionism and performance fears by young adulthood, but they accompanied me, strong and demanding, as I entered motherhood. After all, what could be more important than getting this mothering thing right?

ON-THE-JOB TRAINING

As anticipated, baby Philip made his debut right on time. We encountered a few bumps with bili lights and long nights, but we were finally home. Brad went back to work while I tried not to panic over being responsible for this tiny, squalling human all day by myself. This is what I had always wanted, but now what was I supposed to do?

My perfectionistic tendencies began bullying me as soon as Philip arrived. I was keenly aware of the eternal significance mothering held, and I felt like I had to be ready and on guard at all times. I refused to rest when Philip was an infant even when help was offered because I knew that soon he would need to nurse. I constantly teetered on the brink of frazzled. Brad worked nearby and usually made it home at a decent time, but whenever he called to tell me he would be delayed, even if only by fifteen minutes, I launched into a panicked tailspin. I lived with little physical or emotional margin because of the unrealistic demands I placed on myself.

Not everything was a struggle, though. Like every mom, I figured out some things pretty quickly. Philip slept in a bassinet in our bedroom the first night home, and I was aware of his every grunt and wiggle. Each time I dozed off, I soon woke to a squirm or sigh and jumped up wondering if he was ready to nurse. I never did that again. Philip moved to his own room with no baby monitor. When he needed to eat, he made enough noise to let me know. Problem solved.

However, with no one to coach me and no friends or acquaintances nearby with a baby, there were other tricks I didn't grasp as quickly. Motherhood is an occupation that requires intense on-the-job training and often skill is acquired through learning what *doesn't* work. I definitely made plenty of mistakes to learn from.

As a newborn, Philip fell asleep while nursing. As he got a little older, I thought I had to continue that pattern. He would doze off in my arms, only to wake as I laid him in his crib—no matter how gently I handled him or how much I held my breath. It became a tedious, nightly operation as I repeated the process until he finally slept soundly. I didn't realize I could lay him down awake and expect him to fall asleep on his own.

I also continued nursing him during the night long after he should have slept through. An out-of-town friend arrived shortly after Philip's first birthday and expressed surprise that he still woke to nurse in the wee hours. I tucked that info into my back pocket for the few days she visited, then whipped it out to give it a try. The jig was up. Now that I knew he should be sleeping, sleep he would. The first night after my friend left, when Philip cried, I went in once, gave him his pacifier, and told him to go back to sleep. He halfheartedly fussed for a while, but within a couple of nights, he didn't bother to wake. We both started enjoying a glorious, uninterrupted, restful night.

But I wasn't finished with the blunders. Another mistake I made was weaning him from the breast to a bottle. As soon as our pediatrician pointed out my goof, I began introducing him to the sippy cup. The poor guy didn't know which end was up or where his next drink was coming from. In all these instances, I simply didn't know better.

I pulled off some rookie mistakes, but somehow Philip survived my misguided attempts and motherhood missteps. It's funny to me now. The blunders I made should have been obvious and easy to avoid. But the solutions weren't apparent to me. I had to learn.

GRACE DESPITE MY MISTAKES

During my young adult years—college through early motherhood —I mindlessly absorbed the messages of my culture, embraced some naive assumptions, and made mothering much more difficult than it had to be. I was young and inexperienced.

But I was a mom. God had answered my long-standing prayer and given me a child. Philip's sweet smiles, contagious laughter, and curious wonder delighted me daily. And that delight was not diminished by my mistakes.

I began to realize that despite my ineptitude, the world didn't fall apart, and the Lord never once took aim at that imaginary target on my back. I started where I was, and God met me there. Slowly, I absorbed the truth that my blunders didn't make me "less than" as a mother or as a human; they simply meant that I was a beginner. I dared to shake hands with God's sweet grace.

Through all of this, I did my best to learn from my mistakes and grow in my mothering skills. Almost without being aware of it, I opened my fist just enough to allow a little perfectionism to leak out. I was still very performance-based in my thinking and reactions, still determined to control as much as I possibly could, but the nature of motherhood demanded that I keep moving forward, even when things weren't perfect. I didn't have the luxury of spending a lot of time worrying about how I was doing. Philip was healthy and well under my care, and ultimately, that's what mattered.

WATERED BY THE WORD

In the midst of all I was learning in my new role as a mother, I was given the opportunity to pursue a master's degree at the college where Brad worked. The option sounded wonderful until I considered the time, money, and most importantly, the content of what I would be learning. I had majored in English literature in my undergraduate studies and although I loved most of it, the brokenness and hopelessness of some of the required reading wearied me.

If I was going to invest my limited time and energy, I wanted to be focused on something worthwhile. I wanted to work on what was important to me, not what a professor assigned. I knew my Scripture literacy was deficient, and that was what I was really hungry for. Did I want more listless, lifeless words or the life-giving Word of God? When I looked at pursuing a master's degree from that angle, the answer was easy. The Bible is what I wanted to master. This realization compelled me to find an in-depth Bible study and dig in.

Philip napped in the next room and even though I was sprawled across my bed, I wasn't sleeping. My Bible, a three-ring binder, and several colored pencils littered the smooth, green-and-cream striped comforter. I bit my bottom lip in concentration, marking keywords and making lists while I wrestled with the passage before me. I spent countless naptimes this way—digging into God's Word, finally seeing for myself the riches of Scripture. This was worth the effort of my limited time.

I completed my weekly homework and traveled to Chattanooga every Tuesday. Dad and I attended a Bible study class in the evening while Mom babysat. On Wednesday morning, Philip and I would load up the car and drive the seventy-five minutes back to Rome. It was a rhythm that suited us well and laid a foundation that offered huge benefits. I hungered for God, for answers, for truth. The Scriptures pointed the way to all those riches.

I began to know and trust the Lord in a deeper way. He invited me to witness His beauty and discover the abundance of life lived in dependence on Him. He wooed me gently into a greater awareness of His grace. And slowly God began to change me. No longer did I rely on the opinions of those around me nor was I as easily duped by the current cultural messaging. I learned to stand on the stability of the Word and the God of the Word. Of course, learning and transformation is a lifelong process, but my education had begun. I was growing. It was a huge turning point in my life.

ADDITIONS

About the time Philip turned a year old, my cycles kicked back into gear, and I was once again fertile. We had previously decided not to go back on hormonal contraception, but to use a barrier method instead. We knew we wanted a baby again soon, so we once again began praying about the timing of a possible pregnancy. We decided to wait one more month and then stop using birth control.

I'm not sure why we thought it necessary to wait another month, but we reached our decision and it made sense to us at the time. Being unaware of the finer points of my own fertility I assumed my body followed the textbook timeline of ovulation two weeks after the beginning of my last period. Brad and I both disliked the barrier method, so a few days after the two-week mark in my cycle, we stopped using it. And just like that, baby number two was on his way.

We were thrilled. It had happened a month sooner than we planned, but we set out excitedly to tell friends and family our good news.

Even though I was beginning to be shaped by the freedom and grace God offered, I was still enamored with many of my old habits. I remained a bit high-strung, wanting things just so and worrying about everything that felt out of my control. One thing I stressed over was how this baby's arrival would affect Philip. I mourned that Philip's whole world was about to change, and I didn't anticipate an easy transition. All my fretting and "poor little guy" sighing turned out to be nothing more than overblown, unnecessary drama as Isaac made his debut. Philip adjusted beautifully, and like countless mamas before me, I learned to juggle two squirmy boys on my lap instead of just one. Why had I fretted so much?

Parenting two young sons wasn't easy, but I was learning, and we settled into a fairly manageable routine. I relaxed just enough to admit that I was having fun.

When Isaac turned one, my cycles returned right on schedule. We were busy with the boys, so we had not discussed the possible timing of a third child, and we hadn't taken to heart the lesson offered by Isaac's conception. Thinking that the last time was a fluke, Brad and I once again stopped using our barrier-method birth control just over halfway into my cycle. Once again, the double pink lines made their debut to a surprised but appreciative audience.

I remember feeling the slightest twinge of embarrassment at telling others that I was pregnant again. Three babies in quick succession pushed the culturally acceptable boundary a little, but soon I shed that shyness for the joy of sharing our news.

Before Brad and I married, we knew we wanted a big family. He grew up the sixth of seven children. He loved the boisterous, mischievous mix of lots of siblings. I only had one younger brother, but had always wished for a sister too, and thought a large family would be fun. And as much as I wanted to be a mom, I guess I also wanted to extend that role at long as possible. The only thing better than being a mom would be becoming a mom of many. In our discussions, Brad and I agreed that our definition of a big family included four children, and with our third child now on the way, we were right on schedule.

FAMILY INFLUENCE

Abigail arrived—small, but perfect—exactly three weeks early. The morning of her birth, in a rare moment of hospital quiet, I held her in my arms, her sweet pink face peeking out of her pink blanket. Brad sat dozing on the chair by my bed, exhausted from our night of little sleep. I pressed my face into Abigail's soft head, inhaling her new baby scent and savoring the tickle of her fuzzy hair on my cheek. A soft knock announced the arrival of my grandparents, eager to meet their new great-granddaughter.

A nurse walked briskly in behind them, pushing the hush aside as she entered, and waking Brad in the process. She fluttered around, checking this and adjusting that while Grandmommie and Granddaddy squeezed into the corner. Finally, she exited, taking the whirlwind with her and allowing the quiet to settle in once again.

Granddaddy paused long enough to make sure the door stayed closed before moving toward the bed and perching gingerly on the edge. He gazed at Abigail for a moment, offered his congratulations, and then looked squarely into my eyes. "This is the caboose," he said gesturing toward his sleeping great-granddaughter nestled in my arms.

I breathed in the familiar scent of Granddaddy's signature Old Spice cologne and returned his gaze with a raised eyebrow.

He recognized my confusion and continued, "You have your boys and now you have a girl—so this is it."

When I didn't respond immediately, he pressed. "Right?" My sixty-eight-year-old grandfather furrowed his shaggy eyebrows and leaned back expectantly.

I sought Brad's eyes and found the confirmation of my desires mirrored in his before looking down at our sweet daughter. I laughed self-consciously and pushed Granddaddy's directive aside as politely as possible. "Oh really?" I replied lightly. I wasn't arguing, but I wouldn't agree with him, either.

Granddaddy pressed his lips together briefly but let the issue drop.

The conversation surprised me. It wasn't typical for Granddaddy to offer advice with no discussion or preamble. It occurred to me that he must feel pretty strongly about it to blurt out this declaration so uncharacteristically. But he didn't offer more explanation and I didn't ask.

Granddaddy's urging was utterly opposed to our hopes and

plans. We didn't know what we were doing most of the time, fumbling along as relatively new parents, but one thing we knew was that we wanted more of these precious babies. We had no idea of how long this train should or would be, but we knew we didn't want Abigail to be the caboose. At the very least, we knew we wanted four children, but already our hearts were softening to the possibility of more.

This was a defining moment for Brad and me. Before, we had been swayed by what was culturally acceptable, and now we were being challenged by family members we loved and respected. This time, however, we exercised the freedom of moving beyond others' expectations to embrace a different possibility. If God was willing to give us more children, we were on board.

LETTING GO

Abigail was born twenty months after Isaac, so for a short while, we had three children aged three and under. This time, I didn't stress about how the boys would react when Abigail was born. I knew they would have their moments, but ultimately, they would love their little sister. Life was lively and exhausting and I was beginning to mellow out as a mother. No longer did I refuse help when offered. Even though I still scoured parenting books hoping to find the key to raising godly young men and women (or at least the secret to survival), I began to realize that my children didn't fit into some fixable formula.

I often resisted Brad's coaxing to leave the mess in the house and come out to play with him and the kids, but I began to see the futility of attempting to make life fit into my tidy, perfectionistic maxim that the work must be finished before rest or play. A mother's work is never done, so occasionally I snuck out for fresh air and fun rather than the frantic straightening I typically attempted when my little mess-makers were otherwise occupied.

In addition to mothering skills and a greater grasp of His

Word, the Lord was teaching me in other practical areas during this time. He coaxed me to trust Him for provision as Brad accepted a new job with income based on commission rather than a set salary. With the ebb and flow of business—and consequently our paychecks—we began to understand and more concretely experience God as our provider.

On a more intimate level, one of the things I internalized after each child was an increased awareness of God's love for me. I adored each baby, my heart stretching toward my children in infinite ways. As I contemplated my tender feelings as a mother, I began to catch a glimpse of the incredible affection of God toward me—His child.

One day when Abigail was still an infant, I sat on the couch with her propped on my lap, secured with one arm. My other hand held a book and Philip and Isaac were pressed against me on either side. The boys were uncharacteristically still and drowsy after we read together and Abigail was sleeping deeply. I looked down at her peaceful face, overwhelmed with God's generous blessings to me.

Philip was three, growing and active—becoming more independent and fun. Isaac wasn't yet two, still toddler chubby, his outstretched arms reaching up often to be held. I had a blast interacting with them and enjoying their curiosity and quirks. Abigail was still too young to smile or offer intentional responses to my love and care. But that didn't matter. I loved her simply because she was mine. I loved them all because they were mine. They didn't have to "do" anything. I just loved them as they were. As I gazed at them in this rare moment of stillness, a startling thought crossed my mind. *Could it be that God loves me this way?* I knew in my head that it was true, but I hadn't yet connected that reality in a meaningful way to my heart.

I kissed both of the boys on the head and we sat until Philip roused himself and jumped up to find another book. The moment passed but there were many more epiphany realizations God gave me as I mothered. Meeting the needs of my children and recognizing their helplessness without my care encouraged me to consider my own helplessness before the Lord. As I snuggled with them, I could imagine being held in His secure arms. Just being with them brought me joy and gave me the assurance that I, too, brought joy to my Father.

The wonder of all that never diminished, and each child was a vivid representation of God's tenderness toward me. I eventually moved from a "God has to love me because He has obligated Himself" mentality to a "God actually delights in me beyond what I can imagine" realization. That deepening understanding was one small but eternally significant gift God wrapped up in the sweet little bundles of joy He gave. Every time.

His love also freed me to relax my perfectionistic standards. Maybe my worth was not wrapped up in my works. Maybe I could let go of a false sense of significance based on my performance. And maybe God wasn't looking for an opportunity to use my backside for target practice after all. The Lord didn't love me less in my mistakes, immaturity, and naivety, but neither did He leave me there. One small step after another, He increased my skill, faith, and love. Most importantly, He gave me the grace to begin letting go of the unattainably perfect life I had always struggled for in exchange for a vision of the abundant life He generously offers instead.

These were years of laying the groundwork. Through it all, God patiently and compassionately taught me about mothering, about mercy, and about Himself. He persistently led me along and showed me a better way, guiding me down a generous path of growth and grace. Psalm 71:17 describes my experience: "O God, You have taught me from my youth." From my earliest childhood desires to my early years as a mother, the Lord had been faithfully leading me toward abundance and freedom with Him—toward a beautiful heritage.

The Chosen Ones

EMBRACING THE BEAUTY OF CALLING

Who has saved us and called us with a holy calling, not according to our works, but according to His own purpose and grace which was granted us in Christ Jesus from all eternity.
2 Timothy 1:9

January 22, 1995, was an ordinary Sunday so we did what we ordinarily did. We rushed and cajoled, fed and wiped faces, coaxed shoes on, and re-stocked diaper bags before flying out the door. We arrived at church just in time, then wrangled the kids to their nursery and preschool rooms. Finally, we were free to plop onto the hard-bottomed chairs of our adult Sunday school class.

Before the teacher began his lesson, Lew, the father of our good friend Paige stood to describe God's leading and provision for a new venture in his life. He was going to work full-time opening the local branch of a small adoption agency based out of Portland, Oregon. Lew shared exciting details of God's provision for the new office of All God's Children International (AGCI) and his role there.

As he spoke, Lew mentioned how God had provided the office

space and brought about the relationship that initiated his new position. His focus wasn't on the needs of the orphans he would be serving through AGCI or the relief plans for those children who were unadoptable. He simply pointed out all the ground-work the Lord had laid to make a local office possible.

As I sat, listening to the encouraging words of God's obvious work, the Lord spoke: **This is for you.** Lew's voice faded into the background as I concentrated on that quiet but unmistakable inner communication from my Father. I knew exactly what He meant: adoption.

God had rarely spoken to me so clearly and directly and the wonder of that intimate moment washed over me. I was in awe that He would not only converse with me so personally but also assign a task I eagerly welcomed. It felt like grace upon grace. But I wondered what Brad would think. Would he understand and agree to this calling?

Planted in the chair, I began to pray. *God, this feels too big. I don't want to be the one to bring this up. Would you tell Brad too?* As I poured out my concern to the Lord, Brad squeezed my hand and leaned over. His breath warmed my cheek as he whispered, "I would really like to do that." My heart leapt with gratitude and worship. I looked up at Brad with tear-filled eyes and saw the moisture in his eyes too.

The rest of the morning we went through the motions, but our minds were consumed with thoughts of adoption and whether or not God was calling us to pursue such an adventure. When we arrived home, we sought to clarify the Lord's direction and committed to pray for confirmation of what we both believed we had heard. We wanted more children and were thrilled with the possibility of adoption, but we wanted to make sure we weren't coming up with this whole idea ourselves. We decided to simply seek the Lord, not search out details about the process or what it might cost. We didn't want to be swayed by finances or other considerations.

For the next couple of days, we entreated God for guidance. We prayed separately; we prayed together. We scoured His Word, asking God to confirm His leading in this sweet, unexpected assignment. Adoption was a giant leap in our cautious, conservative world, but I received a settled heart when I read Psalm 27:10: "For my father and my mother have forsaken me, but the Lord will take me up." God assured Brad's heart too. We didn't know how it would play out with money, timing, or any other detail, but we knew we were supposed to pursue it. Within two days, the Lord had moved us from no consideration of adoption to being fully committed.

We didn't have a specific country in mind but felt confident that All God's Children would be the agency we would work through. They were a relatively new agency and had a budding presence in Eastern Europe, so we assumed that is where our child would be from.

I called All God's Children on Thursday, introduced myself to Paul, the director, and explained our interest. The conversation wasn't exactly encouraging.

"Tell me a little about yourself," he prompted while I pulled the phone cord taut, then watched it coil back up. "How long have you been married and do you have children?"

"Brad and I have been married for seven years. We have three children ages four, two, and four months. We are interested in adopting from the eastern European region and are really excited about moving forward with this." My voice trembled a little with nervousness.

Paul didn't bother to soften his reply. "You have too many children to be eligible for our Bulgaria program. The only country we are currently in that would be a fit for you is China." He paused for a moment before continuing.

"But that's not my biggest concern." My heart beat with an uncertain thud as Paul explained. "The ages of your children are an issue. I don't know any social worker in America who would approve your home study." He sighed. "And frankly, out of the eighty adoptions we have facilitated, the only one that failed involved a family with young children."

I remained quiet during his explanation, absorbing what he was saying and wondering where that left us. I finally responded with the only thing I could think to say. "We are sure God spoke to us about this. Please keep us in mind."

Paul's voice was flat. "Call me back when your kids are twelve, ten, and eight if you are still interested. Then we'll see what we can do."

I slowly replaced the receiver, discouraged by the conversation. I wasn't pregnant, but the idea of pursuing adoption had bestowed a conception of the heart that made me *feel* expectant. After this exchange, it seemed as if I had just been informed that I was mistaken—that I wouldn't soon hold another child after all.

My talk with Paul ended abruptly, but I immediately picked up the conversation with God. *Is he right? Are we supposed to adopt sometime in the future?* Part of Isaiah 43:19 leapt into my head: "Now it will spring forth; will you not be aware of it?" I knew God had answered—swiftly and surely. Now was the time to pursue adoption.

Brad and I were faced with the clear tension between what seemed impossible and what God said He would do. We had two choices: we could believe what Paul said and what the circumstances looked like or we could, in faith, hold on to what God said and what He had initiated. The rest of Isaiah 43:19 reassured us: "I will even make a roadway in the wilderness, rivers in the desert." God gave us the grace and encouragement to believe that He would accomplish this despite the obstacles. If He had a child for us somewhere else in the world, nothing could change that.

As we processed through all this, 1 Thessalonians 5:24 also encouraged us. "Faithful is He who calls you, and He also will bring it to pass." This verse became our rallying cry during the months of hurdles ahead.

Over the next couple of days, the whole idea of God bringing this about seemed more and more confirmed in our hearts. At first, we had been reluctant to announce our intentions—especially after Paul's abrupt dismissal. What if we were wrong? What if God didn't really come through? But as we moved forward, we began to trust that a child would join our family as a result of God's work on our behalf.

As a symbolic gesture of faith and with growing excitement, on Saturday evening we purchased an adoption-themed baby book. I sat on the couch after the children were in bed that evening, tracing the embossed lettering and wiping tears from my cheeks before they could drip on the precious pages. As I carefully turned each page, dreaming of the day our child's information would fill the blanks, I realized that I truly believed God would do this. It was no longer a timid "maybe" in my mind, but a settled reality. It might not be easy, but God would accomplish this from start to finish. It was incredible to think that this time last week, adoption wasn't on our radar, but now Brad and I were excited and eager to move forward.

We also chose a name. We had no real reason to think our child would be a girl, but we knew the name fit. We would call her Ruth. It was our earnest prayer that "[our] people [would] be [her] people and [our] God, [her] God," just as Ruth of the Bible had declared to her mother-in-law long ago (see Ruth 1:16).

MADE IN CHINA

The next time we contacted AGCI, Brad was the one who called. Paul was unavailable so we were forced to wait for him to get back to us. I was the one at home when the phone finally rang.

"Hello, Paul. Thank you for returning our call." I said quickly, then plunged ahead before I lost my nerve. "I know you don't want to hear this, but we are confident that now is the time we are supposed to adopt." I twisted the phone cord around my finger so tightly that it began to turn blue.

Paul still sounded hesitant, but he gave me an opening, "Well if that's the case, I guess we'd better pay attention. Tell me about it."

I uncoiled the phone cord with a sigh of relief, encouraged by Paul's response after the previous week's dismissal. God had apparently softened his heart over the last few days. I'm confident that Lew had vouched for us as believers and as parents and maybe Paul also needed to know that we were serious enough to keep pushing. Regardless, now he seemed to accept the possibility that we had heard from God.

Paul explained that the first couple of families were headed to China soon to initiate All God's Children's adoption program there. If everything worked out, we could go as a part of the second group later in the year. After the current adoptions were complete, AGCI would evaluate and see what changes needed to be made to adjust their China application package and advise the adopting families accordingly. He wanted us to wait to begin our paperwork until the adjustments were final.

At first, the idea that our child would be from China surprised us. Until our initial conversation with Paul, we hadn't even known that AGCI had a presence in that country. After he told us it was the only area we were qualified for, we began gathering specific information about China's adoption program. China didn't object to the fact that we had three children, but couples who were already parents could only adopt a "handicapped" child. "Handicapped," was China's wording for a wide range of birth defects, conditions, and ailments, many of which were easily correctible or treatable. Still, finding specialized care (including possible surgery) for a new child felt a little intimidating with three young children in the family who already needed constant care and supervision.

Another interesting quirk about China's adoption program

was that they denied couples the option of choosing a child from among the pool of adoptable children. Instead, the Chinese committee assigned each couple a child based on China's preferences and any additional considerations they obtained from the prospective family's paperwork. While this was hard for some adoptive couples, it didn't bother us at all. We trusted that God knew exactly who He had chosen to join our family and that He would see to it that our child came home with us. There would be no agonizing over multiple photos or videos of children needing parents. We would simply receive some information (and hopefully a picture) when the committee assigned a child to us. One of us would then be required to travel to China to formalize the adoption and accompany our new family member home.

At this time in China's history, the government was stringently enforcing its infamous one-child policy. Couples in most areas were only allowed to raise one child. Second pregnancies subjected parents to large fines, family eviction, or job loss and were often terminated, sometimes even forcibly by the government. Most couples wanted baby boys since sons traditionally took care of their parents as they aged. Tragically, a great number of girls in the years between 1980-2015 were aborted or abandoned so that parents could try again for a boy.[1] This information seemed to confirm that our child would be a daughter.

As we continued to connect the dots in our research, March arrived and AGCI's first group of adopting parents traveled in-country and returned home with their beautiful girls. By this time, we had spoken to those families several times, absorbing every detail. We were encouraged by their safe and successful return to the States, and we waited anxiously to get started with our own process.

WHIRLWIND TWO WEEKS

The AGCI office was tastefully decorated and comfortable. As Brad and I walked through the glass door, the smell of new carpet intertwined with a faint perfume worn by one of the women in attendance. My parents followed us in, eager to understand more of the adoption process.

On Sunday afternoon, April 9, 1995, an official ribbon-cutting ceremony heralded the opening of the Chattanooga office of All God's Children International. Everyone from the Portland headquarters was there. Our pastor attended and spoke a few words. Lew and his wife Sue and our friends Paige and Phillip wove in and out of the crowd, welcoming the local businessman who had donated the space, as well as the many other well-wishers gathered to celebrate.

A few minutes later, Brad and I leaned over several official-looking documents, both of us with slightly shaking hands. Amid smiles and the click of my dad's camera, we signed the contract with AGCI. I scratched out the $4000 check and we both felt our hearts resonate with the release as I tore the slip off its spine. We'd never been so excited for someone to take our money.

Finally, it was time to begin.

Over the next couple of weeks, we blazed through the requirements. All of the pent-up energy and longing we had repressed was directed at the tasks that could now be accomplished—and needed to be accomplished. Our daughter was in China and we were on a mission to bring her home. The days flowed by in a continuous stream of tasks:

April 10: Sort through the requirements and begin paperwork. Order certified copies of birth and marriage certificates.

April 11: Go to local police station to be fingerprinted for the Immigration and Naturalization Service (INS) paperwork.

April 12: First home study appointment. After Paul's initial declaration that no social worker would approve us, we met

Brenda with a little trepidation. Lew had paved the way, affirming that we were capable parents, but we still weren't sure how she would react to our situation. Brenda was difficult to read, but she gave us twenty questions to answer about our marriage plus an outline template for each of us to write an autobiographical analysis. We considered it a win that she didn't refuse to work with us.

April 13: Drop off medical forms at three different physicians' offices: Brad's, mine, and the kids' pediatrician.

April 14: TB tests for us and the kids. Pick up pediatric medical forms. Begin home study questions while children spent a few hours with friends.

April 18: Brad's required physical.

April 19: Finish home study questions.

April 20: Apply for passport.

April 22: Fill out INS paperwork.

April 25: Turn in home study paperwork.

April 26: Send required packet to INS via FedEx.

April 28: Get bank statement and submit to two more criminal checks.

We were driven to finish. Brad and I raced through all the initial paperwork and errands in just over two weeks. Then we hit a hurdle.

OUT OF OUR HANDS

An assistant from the Portland office called to check on our progress. She was pleased we had completed our part and asked us to check with Brenda about the timeline for finishing the home study. AGCI hoped to coordinate all the families currently in process for the China program so that we could travel together as soon as possible.

We reached out to Brenda, who returned our call on Tuesday, May 2. I picked up the phone, glad to hear her voice on the other end of the line and anxious to receive an update. I breathlessly began to tell her that AGCI wanted us to move forward quickly, but Brenda interrupted me.

"I can't work on your file right now," she said brusquely. "Feel free to use someone else."

My mouth fell open, and I groped for some meaningful way to respond. *What is going on?*

When I didn't say anything, Brenda continued in clipped tones. "Lew and I discussed it and thought it would be best to wait a month or two before moving forward." Then she curtly added, "You do have responsibilities toward your other three children, you know."

I swallowed hard and informed her as politely as I could that we would wait for her availability. Then I hung up. I sank onto a nearby kitchen chair, my mind churning. *Perhaps Brenda is becoming apprehensive about recommending us for adoption. Or maybe Lew is entertaining some reservations himself?* Either way, they had apparently had a conversation in which they thought it best to slow things down. Brad and I were unaware of this shift in perspective, and Lew and Brenda had obviously not yet communicated this to the team in Portland either.

After an evening of prayer and discussion with Brad, we decided that I would call Lew the next morning to find out what he was thinking and plead our case. I made the call and pressed as much as I dared. I assured him that we wanted to move ahead immediately, but Lew seemed to be taking a "hold back" approach and hinted that it might not even be this year. Then he took the whole situation out of our hands. *He* would contact the Portland office. *He* would contact Brenda. Everything in me longed to call Portland to advocate for us to move forward *now*, but I knew I couldn't do that. God had used Lew to vouch for us in this process, and we needed to see how the Lord would work through him this time.

I couldn't fix this—couldn't control the outcome or influence the results. My role was to pray and wait. As I put the boys in bed for a nap, I implored God to direct the conversation between Lew and Paul. I entreated Him to work out the best timing as I tucked the covers around wiggly arms and legs. Then, with Abigail on the floor beside me, I flopped down in an anxious heap, realizing the significance of this moment and its direct impact on our daughter who waited for us on the other side of the world.

With no more words to pray, I began quietly singing an old hymn that came to mind:

> Take my life, and let it be
> Consecrated, Lord, to Thee;
> Take my moments and my days,
> Let them flow in ceaseless praise,
> Let them flow in ceaseless praise.[2]

She couldn't comprehend the words, but Abigail gazed steadily at me with her clear blue eyes as I surrendered my hopes, my understanding of what was best, and my desire to fix all of this. I didn't know what had changed Lew and Brenda's opinions. I didn't know how Paul would respond—he was, after all, the one with reservations from the beginning. But slowly a gentle peace coaxed the anxiety from my heart. God had started this and He was certainly big enough to complete it.

Later I learned that shortly after I was singing on the floor, Lew called Paul and explained the reasons he and Brenda thought it best to wait a while. Paul listened to the concerns, but still made the final decision that our family would keep moving forward without delay. I don't know all the details of the conversation, but I know the result: God moved Paul's heart on our behalf. The person who was originally the most skeptical intervened even when others waffled over the wisdom of moving forward quickly. Halleluiah!

On Wednesday, May 17, I spent 45 minutes with Brenda for a

personal interview. It felt awkward at first, but I spoke candidly about all the reasons we wanted to adopt. Brad did the same two days later. The following Monday she came to inspect our house and speak with the friends we had named as references. She seemed pleased with the visit and much more relaxed as she got to know us. Brenda promised to have our home study written up and completed within the week.

On Wednesday, May 31, we escorted our thick pile of paperwork to the Hamilton County Clerk to be certified. Two days later we traveled to Nashville to stand in line at the secretary of state's office for final certification. Early the following week we wrote another check to AGCI and FedEx-ed our documents off to be translated into Chinese and eventually forwarded to Washington. Now, we just needed our INS approval to come through.

CALLED AND CHOSEN

June passed slowly as we dreamed about our daughter and wondered when we would be able to bring her home. We settled back into normal life after the flurry of paperwork and errands and often talked to other couples who had adopted from China, hungry for any information or insight. Calls to the INS to check on the necessary clearance to allow our daughter into the country were slow and frustrating, but we finally retrieved the approval documentation from our mailbox on July 14 and sent it off for translation. We were in the final phase of our paperwork.

As the hectic pace slowed and our ability to push the process along waned, I found myself with more time to ponder all that was happening. The most significant marker of this time was that I carried an acute awareness of God's presence and His good plan in a tangible, specific way. I had experienced a fresh realization of the Lord's love toward me with each of my newborns, but this time the sense of His presence was heady. I couldn't get enough. I poured over His Word—praying and journaling in a notebook so I wouldn't forget one precious realization or direction. I was over-whelmed that the God of this whole universe would take the time to single us out and give us such a beautiful and unexpected gift.

I also had the opportunity to consider some of the implications of adoption as we waited. Adoption, I was learning, isn't about our worthiness or our loveliness or some return on investment we can offer that gives us value. Instead, adoption invites us in when we are at our weakest and neediest. Adoption looks beyond *who* we are and declares *whose* we are.

For those who believe in Christ, our adoption was initiated while we were desperate sinners. We were strangers, separated from God, and without hope (Ephesians 2:12). We could do nothing to make ourselves presentable or worthy. In fact, we were enemies of God before He chose us for life (Romans 5:10). But now, because of Christ's death and resurrection we have been saved and called with a holy calling "according to His own purpose and grace which was granted us in Christ Jesus from all eternity" (2 Timothy 1:9). When we had nothing worthwhile of our own to offer, God still chose to rescue us from our helplessness and give us a name, a family, and a purpose.

To be called is to be invited or summoned. It starts with our "adoption...through Jesus Christ...according to the kind intention of His will" (Ephesians 1:5) and includes an "inheritance which is imperishable and undefiled and will not fade away" (1 Peter 1:4). Belonging to God's family grants us a beautiful heritage guaranteed to last forever. We have the full rights and privileges of beloved sons and daughters with the Holy Spirit as our guarantee. (2 Corinthians 1:22) We are never left on our own —always loved, always wanted, always belonging. Secure in God's love, we are home.

In addition to our eternal standing in God's family, we are also invited into abundant life *now*. That includes a life of purpose. God has called us to holiness (1 Peter 1:14–16), to love (Matthew 22:36-40), and to a life that pleases Him "in all respects" (Colossians 1:10). The Lord also calls us to specific works (Ephesians 2:10) which may include lifetime assignments or more temporary projects. Brad and I were thrilled to have the temporary task of bringing our daughter home and the long-term assignment of parenting her well. Both were gracious callings from the heart of our loving God.

These realizations sustained me during the long, slow weeks of summer as we anticipated the day that the final pieces of our adoption process would fall into place.

NEWS

Finally, at the beginning of August, our dossier was in order and sent to China along with the paperwork for the other three families. It left AGCI on Friday, August 4, and we speculated that by Wednesday the ninth, it would be sitting on some official's desk in far-away Beijing. The countdown had begun. All that was left to do was wait.

At the time, approval of an adoption and assignment of a child was usually a quick two-or-three-week process. That is unheard of today. Now, it's not uncommon for families to wait months or even years for a match once their paperwork is in-country. But on this occasion, it took exactly one week!

I picked up the phone, not really expecting any news about Ruth, but still aware of the subtle twist in my stomach. The twist grew to a full-fledged somersault when I recognized Cindy's breathless voice on the line.

"Are you sitting down?" Paul's wife didn't bother to wait for my response. "The assignments have been made!"

"What?" I gasped as she plowed on.

"They received our papers on August 9 and mailed out the assignments on August 16!" Cindy's voice was almost a squeal. "We don't know any details yet. We haven't received the packet."

"So, you have no idea about the children?" I pressed, images

and questions about our sweet girl flooded my mind and imagination.

"No, but as soon as the packet arrives, we will call you and
also FedEx any pictures that are included."

Cindy barely managed a goodbye before she was off to inform
the other families in our group. I was just as hasty in my call to
Brad. We didn't know the details, but our child had been
assigned!

Two days later, AGCI's assistant called with the information.
Our daughter's given name was Jie and she had been found abandoned in mid-November 1994. Ruth had a cleft lip and cleft
palate that would need to be surgically corrected. She was tiny—
only 14 pounds at nine months old, but otherwise seemed
healthy. When the picture arrived, her smile reached out of the
small, wrinkled photo and wrapped around our hearts.

We all had hoped for and expected a much younger child,
praying her time away from us would have been as minimal as
possible. But we were confident that the Lord had watched over
and provided for Ruth from birth. "For my father and my mother
have forsaken me, but the Lord will take me up" (Psalm 27:10).
This was the child the Lord had chosen for our family and we
were thrilled. We joyfully sent word of our acceptance of Jie
(Ruth) to China. All that was left was to receive an official travel
invitation from Beijing.

If I had thought waiting was difficult before, knowing who she
was made it agonizing. Ruth had been in an orphanage almost all
of her young life. I was her mother and I was coming, but she had
no awareness of me—no understanding, and no hope. Even
though this adoption was moving quickly, the separation seemed
excruciatingly slow. Usually, an invitation arrived within a week
or two after acceptance of the assignment of a child. But Beijing
didn't seem to feel the same sense of urgency we did.

So, we waited. And prayed.

And waited some more.

WAITING AGONIES

A faint sunrise glow peeked through the window as I lay in bed attuned to the distinctive hum of a jet far above the house. Previously, the drone of a plane engine was insignificant background noise that my brain filtered out, but now my ears caught the sound without fail. My yearning flew over the clouds with the jet and on to Atlanta, where the people on board would connect to flights all over the United States and the world. We had waited three weeks for word that I could travel. I sighed and scooted across the sheets. That same early-morning Delta flight from Chattanooga would likely be the first leg of my journey toward China—toward Ruth. She waited… not knowing. I waited…. knowing she was without me. Knowing she needed her mother.

During these weeks of waiting, we continued to converse with other parents who had adopted from China. While our conversations were typically encouraging, I eventually heard something startling. I was warned that sometimes when parents arrived in-country, they were given a different child than the one assigned. That possibility haunted me.

It even disturbed my dreams. One morning, I woke, agitated and breathing hard. It took a few seconds for me to realize I was home in my bed—still waiting. The dream was hazy at first, but I realized I was in China. A man had handed me a baby, and I clasped her to my chest, overwhelmed and relieved to have her in my arms. Finally, I drank her in with my eyes but dismay crowded out the delight in my heart. This child wasn't my Ruth. She wasn't the spunky girl who smiled at me from the picture. Still clutching the child I had been handed, I tried to communicate with the man who was in charge. He didn't understand my frantic gestures, so I ran out of the building and began my search. I had to find her. I would gladly take this baby home too, but I had to find Ruth. I searched frantically until waking brought relief.

The nightmare was an accurate reflection of my concern. Ultimately, I knew God would give me the right daughter, but now that I had Ruth's picture, I couldn't imagine not bringing home the dark-eyed, cleft-lipped cutie I had memorized by heart.

The expected two-week wait dragged into six weeks because of the UN World Conference on Women held in Beijing on September 4–15. No invitations were issued until that conference was complete. Finally, we received the precious summons and finished our last-minute packing, making sure we had everything Ruth would need for the trip home. On October 1, the jet engines roared as I took off from Chattanooga to connect with the other adopting families in Los Angeles. Three hours later, we were in the air over the ocean on our way to Hong Kong and eventually boarded a late evening flight into Hangzhou where we settled into our hotel for a short night of sleep.

EMBRACING RUTH

The morning after we arrived, I woke and rushed to the window. Heavy clouds hung low and wept a constant drizzle, but my eyes widened as I looked down. Spread out on the street below me was an ocean of bobbing color. Thousands of cheerful umbrellas and rain jackets undulated with the footsteps of thousands of people. The view was magical in its enormity and its juxtaposition of bright hues beneath a dreary sky. This was my first glimpse of China.

After a hurried breakfast, we took a couple of cabs to the Ministry of Civil Affairs office in Hangzhou, the capital of Zhejiang Province where our children resided. Our group was composed of a couple, a woman who had brought a friend to help and two moms who had traveled alone—including me. Four new daughters would go home with us.

As we entered the imposing office building, we were cordially greeted by two women in suits and smiles and led to a conference room with a long, oval table and a few scattered chairs around the perimeter. Dark, heavy curtains covered the windows. One too-small clock hung stoically, dwarfed by the otherwise blank wall. The only other decoration in the room was a Chinese flag standing proudly over the proceedings.

The officials overseeing our adoptions brought in hot tea and set a thick stack of papers before us. I sipped the steaming liquid nervously, my teeth closed to block the loose leaves from slipping down my throat. I signed documents along with the rest of the group and wrote a statement detailing why I wanted to adopt a Chinese child.

A young woman entered the room, carrying a baby. The child looked about the same age as our daughter, but she was not my Ruth. The new mama *oohed* and *ahhed* over this sweet girl while hugs and congratulations swirled all around the room. Next, a crying two-year-old was pried out of the arms of her familiar care-giver and enveloped in the lap of her coaxing mom. Finally, a six-year-old arrived. Understanding glimmered in her eyes, but she was pale and hesitant under the weight of this drastic life change. Three of the four girls were now in the custody of their families.

Once again, I was forced to wait. Ruth's orphanage was a greater distance away from the government buildings in Hangzhou, so she wouldn't arrive until the following day. Pushing down my disappointment, I focused on the other girls and how they seemed to be adapting while imagining what it would be like to finally hold Ruth in my arms. After a few more formalities, we all left the building together—the other moms shepherding their children, and me, helping as needed, and sighing over this final delay.

Early the next morning our group returned to the Ministry of Civil Affairs office to wait for Ruth and complete the adoption process for all the girls. A woman in her early twenties entered the room, followed by a thin man wearing a casual blue jacket and a large silver watch. My eyes swept quickly over them and landed on the child in the woman's arms—my Ruth. I will never forget the first time I saw her. She was dressed in a bright yellow sweater with large white buttons. Her pants were striped with dotted long johns peeking out below her knees. Her socks were blue. Ruth's hair stuck straight up—adorned with a tiny red bow.

I reached for her. Ruth grinned and wiggled, coming to me without hesitation as the woman leaned my way. She wasn't afraid or disconcerted about being in a new place with new people. She was simply thrilled with the attention.

On Friday, October 6, 1995, almost nine months after God first spoke to us about adoption, I held my daughter for the first time.

I clasped her tightly, her hair tickling my nose as I breathed in the unfamiliar scent of her formula mingled with baby shampoo. I closed my eyes to savor the moment. The months of God working on our behalf, the pages and pages of paperwork, and all the weary waiting had culminated in this triumph. Our daughter was finally in my arms.

Slowly I become aware again of my surroundings—the woman smiling at me over Ruth's head, the other parents surrounding us with congratulations and pats on the back. Eventually, the room quieted and the woman from the orphanage pressed a glass bottle into my hand with a large hole cut into the attached nipple. A small ziplock bag held some formula and rice cereal. The woman quietly gave instructions for Ruth's feeding times and sleeping habits. She seemed genuinely pleased for Ruth and anxious to make sure I was aware of her immediate needs and routine.

The man who had accompanied Ruth and the young woman was introduced to me as the head of the orphanage in Jiande. His English was broken so we didn't exchange many words but he smiled frequently and also seemed pleased over Ruth's adoption.

The official ceremony followed. I sat at the long table, teacup pushed aside, with Ruth on my lap. My hand trembled slightly from my nervousness and Ruth's wiggles as I signed several more documents. Next, I pressed my finger into red ink to make a fingerprint impression beside my signature. I was told to do the same with Ruth's foot on the paper. Finally, we stood for a picture next to the flag and formal congratulations from the officials.

And just like that, Ruth became a Hinchman. She was ours.

After we returned to the hotel, I bathed Ruth and looked her over carefully, just as a new mom inspects her baby from head to toe. Her legs were thin and stiff in my hands. I caressed her rough skin, trying to avoid the chapped, red patches across her back and on her arms. As I washed her unruly hair, I was alarmed to realize that the back of her head was completely flat. After a few moments of anxiety, I decided the flatness had probably been caused by countless hours of laying on her back in a crib. (Later we would realize that it was actually a birth defect.)

Ruth's eyes were a beautiful liquid chocolate, so dark that her iris was almost indistinguishable from her pupil. Every time our eyes met, she wiggled all over with excitement. Her whole body responded to the rare, longed-for attention and revealed her hunger for connection. I assumed the orphanage workers had done all they could for Ruth, making sure she was fed and clothed. But it was obvious she hadn't had a lot of personal inter-action. Her eyes constantly searched for contact with mine.

Ruth didn't realize that God was the One Who saw her first. His seeing and knowing led to action. He graciously connected us —this once abandoned child with a family and our family with a new daughter. Truly, He had set the "lonely" in a home (Psalm 68:6).

The Lord regards us in the same way. Despite our sin, our shame, and our helplessness He doesn't look away in disgust. Jesus shed His blood to offer forgiveness and mercy. His eyes speak acceptance and invitation. We are known and loved. When we surrender to His delightful summons, He welcomes us into His family. We inherit abundance. We belong. If we realized the full import of that, we would wiggle all over with joy too.

A NEW STORY

"Lucky baby! Lucky baby!" Over and over the phrase followed us as we walked through the crowded streets of China.

I held Ruth in a front carrier, her face to my chest and her thin calves sticking out of the leg holes. We wove in and out of an endless tapestry of curious people. Women touched, women scolded, women tucked and re-tucked Ruth's blanket around her against the cool October air. And always their eyes darted from American mom to Chinese baby.

"Lucky baby!" This time the phrase came from a man with grey hair and a slightly stooped posture. He made the effort to find Ruth's face then looked up at me with startled eyes. "Why didn't you get a pretty one?" His English was clipped, his tone disapproving.

I turned my body to position myself as a shield between this insulting questioner and my daughter. "I did get a pretty one!" I insisted, frustrated that he couldn't see past Ruth's cleft to her playful grin and twinkly eyes. I pushed my way past him, weaving through the throng until Ruth was safely away from his inappropriate attention.

Discouraged, I paused, weary of the questions, the tugging and pulling, the constant correction implying that I didn't know how to properly care for a child. It wasn't only the rude man that had frustrated me, but also the conflicting assumption that Ruth was crazy lucky even though I was hopelessly incompetent. Mostly I was homesick—longing to take Ruth to Tennessee and be united with the rest of our family. It was time to take my daughter home.

With our other three children, I had gasped with relief and praise when they exited my body and lay warm on my chest. I didn't have that privilege with Ruth. I wasn't able to hear and respond to her newborn cries. I hadn't been able to reassure her that she was loved, that she was wanted, that she was precious.

I wasn't there at the moment of her birth. That wasn't our story.

But adoption makes way for a new story.

Adoption is a beautiful reconciliation, offering hope and promise. It is a powerful, persuasive force standing firm in a world enamored with abortion. But adoption only comes out of loss: Loss of connection with birth parents. Loss of what should have been. In Ruth's case, loss of close identity with her birth country and culture. Adoption offers tremendous gain and healing but first came the death of what should have been. It is a gracious response to some of the most wretched brokenness in our world.

When God called us to adopt Ruth, He also called Ruth to join our family. She was born half a world away, but God decreed that she would be a Hinchman. He gave her black, silky hair and almond eyes then plunked her down in Chattanooga, Tennessee where she would have a southern USA childhood with an abundance of playful siblings and imperfect parents. I don't pretend to know the why behind those specific choices, but I am confident that the Lord has been weaving all of Ruth's history together in just the right way for His purposes. Her story threaded into our story becomes a tapestry of purpose and beauty in God's gracious hands.

Ultimately all of our stories have meaning and beauty because they are intertwined with God's story. We "are a chosen race, a royal priesthood, a holy nation, a people for *God's* own possession, so that [we] may proclaim the excellencies of Him who has called [us] out of darkness into His marvelous light" (1 Peter 2:9). We are chosen—rescued from darkness and despair. We are adopted—embraced as beloved sons and daughters. We are called —invited into a life of abundance and purpose. Our story woven into the eternal arc of His story is the foundation of our beautiful heritage.

1. Qingfeng Wang, "Missing Women, Gender Imbalance and Sex Ratio at Birth: Why the One-Child Policy Matters," *Munich Personal RePEc Archive*, mpra.ub.uni-muenchen.de/95412/ MPRA Paper No. 95412, posted 3 August 2019 10:42 UTC

2. Havergal, Frances R. "Take My Life, and Let It Be." (1874)

A Leap of Faith

EMBRACING THE BEAUTY OF TRUST

Blessed is the man who trusts in the Lord,
And whose trust is the Lord.
Jeremiah 17:7

When I finally got off the plane in Chattanooga, I juggled Ruth and her diaper bag down the zigzagging sky bridge and into a chaotic welcome. (Remember when family used to be able to meet you at the gate?) Brad enveloped us both in a bear hug, tear-wet face pressed against his new daughter's cheek. Our other children crowded around, Philip eagerly grasping Ruth's foot, Isaac exclaiming over her thick, black hair, and Abigail clutching my leg, happy to have Mom home and oblivious to her new status as slightly older sister. My parents squeezed in next, rubbing Ruth's back, and then a mass of friends surrounded us with congratulations while their children wove in and out of the chair rows and skipped around the group, munching on the Baby Ruth candy bars our kids had given out in honor of their new sibling.

To my surprise, there was a camera crew from a local news station waiting for us in the terminal. After the initial welcoming

ruckus, the lead reporter asked us for an interview. We sat at the
gate on the curved airport chairs, children in laps and leaning
against us, while the reporter took a chance on our oldest child.

"How many brothers and sisters do you want?" The reporter
stuck a microphone in front of four-year-old Philip, hoping for an
engaging (or at least, discernable) reply. Philip, always ready to
interact with others, didn't disappoint. "Ten boys and ten girls!"
he declared boldly, and we all laughed at his enthusiasm and big-
heartedness. Even though our family size never reached Philip's
ideal of ten boys and ten girls, on that day, I never would have
imagined that we would end up with a generous six and six.

A SURGERY AND A STORK

We were still somewhat flabbergasted that God had called us to
adopt and had ushered Ruth into our family so quickly. We now
boasted four kids ages four and under with all the taxing and
wonderful chaos that entailed. It may seem counterintuitive, but
Brad and I were already eager for another child. We delighted in
each precious newborn, created by God with the capacity to grow
into a life of meaning and purpose. We loved watching each child
develop and stretch toward greater understanding and maturity.
Even though we weren't far past the parenting start line, every
stage promised a new adventure, and we were awed to lead our
children through and experience each phase with them.

We loved being with our little tribe and couldn't imagine
calling Ruth the caboose. Not every day was roses and romance,
of course. But even though our life was challenging, we were
thriving. We recognized the honor and joy of parenting these
precious ones who had been entrusted to us. Parenting was a
significant part of the calling God had placed on our lives and He
always seemed to stretch our capacity and desire for more. It was
as simple and illogical as that.

Abigail and Ruth had both passed the milestone of their first birthdays, and so far, that was typical timing for us to be expecting our next bundle of joy. Since we were facing some challenging surgeries for Ruth in the upcoming months as well as the normal adjustments of adding a child to the family, we reluctantly concluded that it wasn't a good time to try for a baby.

A little sadly, we tucked that desire away for another day. But despite the consistent pattern of our past pregnancies, I had not yet learned my lesson. Why didn't I realize by then that I tended to ovulate a bit later in my cycle than the norm? Twice we had been surprised by conceptions when I thought my window of fertility had passed for the month. Once again, we were caught off guard as the stork circled our neighborhood. The same morning we took Ruth into the hospital for her most complicated surgery (to correct the skull deformity I had noticed on our first night together in Hangzhou), we realized that the friendly bird was hanging around just for us.

We giggled and glowed over our secret—a welcome respite in the middle of a tense, anxious morning. Brad and I couldn't have been more excited even though we weren't sure how the next few months would play out. We knew that ultimately, we would survive the difficulties, and we were thrilled that God was giving us a sweet new addition to the family. The wonder of another baby eclipsed our anxiety over the difficulties we were facing.

Six days after entering the hospital, Ruth was released, with splints on her arms to keep her from tugging at her wounds and instructions to have her sleep in an infant car seat for several weeks. I knew I had roughly one more week before the pregnancy sickness kicked in, so we prepared the best we could—freezing meals, helping the children resume a typical routine, and taking care of Ruth as she healed.

I won't pretend the next several months were easy. I was miserable, Ruth was trying to recover and adjust to her new limitations, and we needed lots of help. My parents pitched in as much as they were able, of course, and our church family also offered large amounts of assistance. There were meals and babysitting and prayers in abundance. And not just for a week or two. Those sweet saints dug in and committed to being the hands and feet of Christ for a couple of months. We limped along, aided and loved until my sickness started abating and it was time for Ruth's last surgery.

WHO'S IN CONTROL?

One day, in the middle of those challenging, chaotic early months of pregnancy, my mother commented that it seemed like an awful time to be expecting. From the outside looking in that was an understandable assessment, and Brad and I had previously come to the same conclusion ourselves when we were considering adding another baby. But now, even though these weeks were difficult, we were amazed at how God had neatly sandwiched my pregnancy sickness between two major surgeries. We couldn't have planned it that way no matter how hard we tried. We had wanted another baby, but we didn't see any way to pull it off with everything happening in our lives right then. God used the timing of this child's conception to get our attention and point to the obvious: our attempts to orchestrate the "suitable" arrival of children hadn't worked, but the Lord knew exactly what He was doing.

Three of our four pregnancies were technically unplanned (by us), though each time we were ready and excited about having another child. With our second pregnancy, if we had followed our initial plan to try for a baby the following month, we might have conceived, but we wouldn't have Isaac. The particular combination of sperm and egg that formed our son would not have been possible a different month. When Abigail was conceived, we hadn't even started the conversation yet. Once Ruth was safely home, we began to long for another child, but we were trying to do the "responsible" thing by not juggling pregnancy sickness during a crazy, demanding spring. In all these instances, God was gracious and gave us children anyway, despite our arbitrary, haphazard, and pseudo-sensible approach to family building.

So that begged the question: Why were we struggling so much, attempting to figure out what was the right time to try for a child, when God was obviously much better at knowing the answer to that than we were? If He is really sovereign (and He is), if children are really blessings (and they are), then perhaps we could trust God to give children in the timing He knew was best. Maybe Brad and I could just get out of the way and stop trying to control what we weren't doing a good job of controlling anyway.

The thought percolated for a while in my heart and spirit, and it seemed to make more and more sense. At this point, however, my only exposure to a family who didn't use birth control was an unflattering comment I'd heard before we had children.

In a passing conversation, a friend had mentioned a couple who wasn't using contraception and my friend thought the wife wasn't completely sold on the idea. Nothing else was alluded to, but I envisioned an oppressed, haggard mom devoid of color, energy, and joy. I'm not sure why that picture popped into my mind, but that was the impression I carried despite my love and desire for children. Now as I ponder my initial reaction, I'm overwhelmed by the contrast of that mental picture with the vibrant, full life that God has given us as Brad and I have followed Him on just such an adventure.

I'm not suggesting that every believing family is obligated to bear as many children as they are physically able. God can lead each couple as He sees fit—in childbearing and all other issues. Abundance comes from following as God leads—moving by faith and entrusting ourselves to the One Who is faithful. An abundant life isn't a life of ease. Nothing about parenting one child is easy, let alone parenting many, but John 14:6 assures us that "Jesus is the way, the truth, and the life." He is the means of our salvation and everything we need—at all times, in every endeavor. He is our sufficiency, and I believe, part of His grace toward Brad and me was giving us the desire for more children even when we couldn't yet fathom the logistics of raising them. My misguided impression of a haggard, dreary existence without the benefit of birth control failed to factor in the Lord's overflowing "enoughness," and as Brad and I continued down this road, we would discover God's sufficiency and abundance in ways we never could have imagined.

AN EXPANDED UNDERSTANDING OF PRO-LIFE

God's Word repeatedly tells us that children are a gift and a blessing. There is room to suggest that we, as believers, have not taken that truth to heart, especially in contemporary times. As young parents, Brad and I followed along with the societal expectation that children should be limited and spaced appropriately, yet it seemed that if we truly agreed with the Lord's assessment that children are good gifts from a benevolent Father, we would be more willing to receive those gifts on His timeline and His terms.

As we anticipated the birth of our fifth child, Brad and I were beginning to question our compulsion to put boundaries on how and when we received that blessing. During the months we were thinking and praying through all this, we began to catch a vision of how we, as a couple, might press more fully into what it means to honor life.

Perhaps being pro-life wasn't simply about holding an anti-abortion stance. Perhaps a "for" life position could include embracing and valuing the precious babies God creates in a mother's womb rather than attempting to prevent them. We couldn't have articulated it exactly like this at the time, but the blessing of our babies and our awe at the privilege of adoption had laid a foundation of growth toward a greater pro-life posture. Like most worthwhile ideas, it would take time to fully develop and produce a genuine conviction in our lives, but it was a start and we were excited to move forward with the vision God was birthing in our hearts.

Becoming aware of these things—God's sweet gift of children despite our attempts at control, our son Samuel's perfectly timed conception between Ruth's surgeries, the obvious account of the Lord's character and sovereignty in Scripture, and the budding comprehension of a deeper pro-life understanding—nudged us to respond to God's gentle invitation. By faith, we entrusted this tender part of our hearts and lives to His benevolent care.

We took the leap of faith and discarded our birth control for good.

At this point, it probably seemed like we were either certifiably nuts or "super spiritual" for handing God the reins in this intimate area of our lives. Really, neither is true. Faith requires moving in the direction God leads without knowing exactly where that will take us. We experienced the usual wavering between confidence and fear that accompanies any significant decision. We wanted more children and, for the most part, felt relieved to no longer be responsible for trying to figure it all out. We didn't have to spend lots of energy deciding if this was an ideal time for a child. We just rested in the fact that God knew best and welcomed each pregnancy with joy and anticipation.

REASSURANCES

Around the time we came to this conclusion, we reconnected with friends from college who had recently moved into town. To our surprise, the Lord had been leading them in a similar manner. The decision to avoid birth control is not a common (or necessarily welcome) one among our friends, and I believe the Lord used us to mutually encourage one another while this determination felt new and radical.

My friend Kim and I had both given birth a few times, so we were able to compare notes. On one such occasion, we chatted in my front yard, our children playing contentedly, drawing on the sidewalk with chalk and dangling from low tree limbs.

"My cycles don't resume until roughly a year after having a baby." My words sounded bright, reassuring me of the suitability of our resolve. "By then we are in a fairly stable routine as a family, and Brad and I are both eager to be pregnant again." As the words came out of my mouth, I realized how deeply I meant them. Our children were unqualified blessings and I loved being their mom. Our joy seemed to multiply as our family grew.

"My cycles start at four months. Like clockwork." Kim spoke slowly, eyes wide and lips forming a tremulous smile. "But God knows how to work that out."

I reached over and squeezed her hand. This was new territory for both of us. We felt honored that the Lord would call us to follow Him in this, but still a bit apprehensive about what it all meant.

At that moment, neither of us knew what the outcome of our obedience would be, but Brad and I realized that Steve and Kim's commitment required more faith than ours. The idea of becoming pregnant only four months after giving birth sounded a lot scarier than our typical scenario. Our decision required faith, but in many respects, it lined up with what we desired anyway—we wanted more children and we liked the spacing that had so far been our norm.

Despite God's leading and His gracious assurances, my heart would occasionally beat wildly and I would find myself breathless at the audacity of what we were doing. It was a big decision with big implications. What if God gave us twelve children or something outrageous like that? Had I known that's where we would end up, I might have buckled to overwhelming fear. But God lovingly led us to follow Him one moment at a time, one day at a time, and one baby at a time.

While our decision was still young enough to wobble and waffle on toddler legs, I continued to seek reassurance from the steady hand of Scripture that we were on the right path. We stepped out with a shaky faith and the Lord was gracious to guide us to solid ground. Reading in 1 Chronicles, I came across a long list of men who served as gatekeepers in the house of the Lord. I furrowed my brow, dutifully plowing through the unfamiliar names, not suspecting that the Lord would meet me in this unlikely passage. "Obed-edom had sons: Shemaiah the firstborn, Jehozabad the second, Joah the third, Sacar the fourth, Nethanel the fifth, Ammiel the sixth, Issachar the seventh, and Peullethai the eighth; *God had indeed blessed him*" (1 Chronicles 26:4–5, emphasis added).

Tucked in that record of tongue-twisting names was a jewel that calmed my heart. Obed-edom had eight sons and God called that blessing. It was a simple statement that I lingered over, finger pointing at the proof until it soaked into my bones. This wasn't just a general "children are a gift and reward" type passage. Although I affirm Psalm 127:3 with all my being, I appreciated the individual emphasis of this account. This was a specific man at a specific time who had eight specific sons. God gave those boys as blessing and they were received that way. Each one held an important place in Obed-edom's family and in the Lord's good plan.

God wasn't trying to trick us into trusting Him just so He could maliciously wreak havoc in our lives. The gift of a child is just that—a gift—with incredible nuances and a lifetime of relationship. No doubt, parenting is a multi-faceted and complicated endowment, but God intends to bless us as we partner with Him to shepherd our children and grow God's kingdom.

FAITH INVITES CHALLENGES

Taking a step of faith in any direction will always have its challenges—both internal and external. The doubts and waffling I walked through are common. I wrestled with so many questions: *Did God really lead in this way? Are we crazy? Will things work out okay?* Internal uncertainty can undermine even the stoutest of intentions when the external pressures roll in.

Moses must have felt that way as he faced Pharaoh. Exodus 1–3 tells us that the Egyptian ruler had enslaved the Israelites and murdered their male babies. God heard and saw the misery of His people and sent Moses to Pharoah to demand the liberation of the Israelites. Moses, filled with doubt, balked at the Lord's command and begged God to send someone else (Exodus 3:10–4:16), but eventually, Moses and his brother Aaron obeyed the Lord and approached Egypt's ruler. The encounter immediately backfired. Instead of Pharaoh agreeing to let the Israelite slaves go, he added more weight to their misery (Exodus 5).

Then Moses experienced pushback from the very people he was trying to help. Their burden was multiplied after his intervention, so naturally, they didn't want any more of his assistance (Exodus 5:20–21). The Bible records Moses' confused prayer: "O Lord, why have You brought harm to this people? Why did You ever send me? Ever since I came to Pharaoh to speak in Your name, he has done great harm to this people, and You have not delivered Your people at all" (Exodus 5:22,23). Like Moses, we can all relate to the dance of doubt that throbs with the beat of our uncertain hearts.

Moses couldn't imagine the magnificent display of power that lay on the other side of his crisis of faith. The Lord would perform signs and wonders and then deliver His people on dry ground through the Red Sea (Exodus 7–14). This would become one of the great milestones of biblical history. In the generations to come, God would refer to His mighty rescue over and over to bolster His peoples' faith and remind them of His faithfulness: "I am the Lord your God who brought you out of the land of Egypt, out of the house of slavery" (Exodus 20:2).

But all that was yet to come. In the midst of his doubts, Moses chose to listen to God and return to Pharaoh again and again, even when it didn't make sense and seemed to be accomplishing nothing but misery. He moved forward in faith, pushing through the difficulties and doubts, obeying the word of the Lord.

PREGNANCY SICKNESS AND PRENATAL SWEETNESS

Like Moses, Brad and I wrestled with difficulties and doubts too. In addition to our natural, occasional qualms, one of the immediate complications we encountered with every pregnancy was the sickness. I don't mean I was a little queasy. I experienced all-day, every-day debilitating nausea until it finally began to subside early in the second trimester. Each morning I crept to the couch, firmly rooted there until I needed to throw up or rescue a child from calamity. Brad worked during the day and returned home each evening to find a desperate wife and hungry children. He would quickly scrounge up some kind of supper for all of us, then tend to the children as best he could. Both of us were barely holding on.

I sat at our round oak table one afternoon after a particularly difficult week. My pregnancy-heightened sense of smell forced me to push away the glass in front of me, as the odor of the water invaded my nostrils and assaulted my already churning stomach. Everything I ate that day had come back up and my throat was raw from the repeated vomiting. I mentally considered and rejected every food I could think of, trying in vain to figure out something I could keep in my rebellious stomach. Giving up, I reverted to the desperate pleading that seemed to be as common as my nausea. *God, please, please remove this awful sickness. It would only take one word from You. I'm so miserable and exhausted. Hasn't this lasted long enough? Please!* I slouched over the table, tears seeping, hands shaking, and nausea entrenched. God remained silent, while my inner turmoil ping-ponged between avid pleas and adamant proclamation: *I can never do this again. I can never do this again!*

With each pregnancy, I made multiple, similar declarations in my distress, and I meant every word. I couldn't imagine surviving and finally leaving behind the awful nausea only to willingly do it again a couple of years later with another pregnancy. After weeks of vomiting and weight loss, recovering strength and putting on weight required weeks too. It was not a fun cycle.

But pregnancy also held wonder and joy. After the nausea finally subsided, I thoroughly enjoyed my maternal state. I felt strong and beautiful in the latter part of pregnancy, but that wasn't the best thing about it. Feeling our babies moving inside of me—the amazing confirmation of active life—was my favorite part of being pregnant. Sharing those moments with our family only increased my enjoyment. One evening during my last trimester, our little guy was especially active. I called Brad and the kids over to witness his antics. As the baby moved, I could feel the sharp jab of his elbow and the pressure caused by his stretching and pressing his whole body against my side. The sensations I experienced on the inside were mirrored in the rolling and tumbling of my belly on the outside. We all gazed, fascinated to see what our baby would do next. I gave him a gentle poke and we laughed when he answered back with his own nudge. We all loved these bonding moments with our newest family member and often gathered to experience the excitement together.

Of course, pregnancy eventually ends with the final struggle of labor, but the lasting reward is a sweet newborn. Like most worthwhile things in life, there is hardship mixed with the beautiful. For me, the intensity of the joy of welcoming a new family member overshadowed the intensity of my misery during pregnancy. No matter how vehemently I claimed I never wanted to be pregnant again, I always changed my tune when the nurse lay my new son or daughter across my chest. The pain I experienced in my pregnancy sickness and labor was real, but the joy I experienced in holding each new baby far eclipsed the agony that had come before. With every birth, I acknowledged that the reward far outweighed the cost. Each precious child—each precious life —was worth it.

PEOPLE PRESSURE

Another interesting external obstacle to abandoning birth control in favor of welcoming any babies God might give, involved the reactions of other people. At the time of our decision, a three-child limit seemed to form the boundary of what was socially acceptable. In our case, we were given grace for a fourth because she was adopted and that was considered altruistic. But this child's conception crossed a line. We became the kook family with all the kids. After two or three children spaced fairly close together, the jokes had begun. *Don't you know what causes this? There must be something in the water at your house.* Then the pressure intensified. *You're not seriously thinking of having more are you? How will you feed all these children? And think of what it will cost to educate them.* The comments came from multiple directions, steadily increasing in number and volume.

Misunderstanding (and often outright opposition) is not uncommon when you follow God's leading in faith—no matter the particulars. And I'm not just referring to unbelievers. I would love to assume that we, as disciples of Jesus, can give each other the grace of realizing that His specific purpose or calling does not look the same in every life. But it's amazing how one couple's decision can make others uncomfortable and uncharacteristically outspoken.

Most of the time comments were voiced out of true (albeit

misguided) concern. A couple of times, though, we were the target of unconcealed contempt.

We walked out of a pizza joint late one afternoon, the sun warm even though the air remained nippy. The kids jostled and tumbled through the door as Brad held it wide and I led the way to our van. A woman walked by our crew on her way to enter the restaurant, mouth open as she counted the bobbing heads.

"Are they all yours?" she asked, eyes wide and one eyebrow raised.

I stopped to reply while Brad took the baby from my arms and marched the kids forward to begin the car seat buckle-rama. "Yes, they're ours."

"I'm *so sorry!*" Her words bit sarcastically, her face a sneer of disgust.

Taken aback by her vehemence, I still managed a tight smile and said sweetly, "I'm not." Then for good measure, I let her in on a secret that wasn't yet obvious. "Oh, and I'm expecting again." I raised my chin and narrowed my eyes before huffing my way back to the van.

After the initial surge of anger, Brad and I just laughed it off, thankful that the children hadn't heard her hateful remark. It did amaze me though, that someone would feel the need to upbraid a total stranger over family size. A friend's mother-in-law also held similar strong opinions. Upon hearing of one of our later pregnancies, she commented that there was more than one way to abuse a child—insinuating that the number of our children alone constituted some kind of neglect.

The comments of strangers and acquaintances stung at times, but worse was the disapproval of family. I've already mentioned my Granddaddy's visit to the hospital to insist that Abigail be the caboose. He and Grandmommie never again rejoiced with us over a pregnancy. They always enjoyed our new babies after birth but made their disapproval clear when pregnancies were announced. They expressed fear that something would happen to Brad, and I would be left to raise the children on my own or that my health would break. Part of it was likely a generational response. They were older and had lived through many difficult experiences and losses that had, perhaps, taught them to be cautious in our unstable world. Maybe they had other reasons they never divulged as well, but ultimately, they didn't approve of our choice nor understand why we would make it.

My parents, on the other hand, always celebrated with us. In fact, informing them of a new pregnancy became quite a tradition. Brad and I always told the kids first, then we all plotted how we would break the news to Mom Mom and Grandpa. It always involved a certain Minnie Mouse shirt that I had worn often during my pregnancy with Philip and usually a poster or two. We would show up unexpectedly at their house, one of us wearing the shirt and several holding signs such as "Eight is great, but nine is FINE!" or "#10–blessed again!"

The kids never failed to be thrilled by another sibling on the way. They would literally shout in excitement and beg to tell all their friends at church. Brad and I enjoyed the privilege of telling the children and my parents, but seldom had the opportunity to share our good news with anyone else. Once the kids started talking, word spread quickly.

After a momentary sting, the negative comments of strangers and even the disapproval of my grandparents simply became background noise. God had led us on this adventure and we were rich, rich, rich for having followed Him. We loved our children and we loved our life. Each child was a treasure, made in the image of God, and—wonder of wonders—entrusted to us. We felt amazingly, abundantly blessed.

FURTHER STEPS OF FAITH

Despite my pregnancy sickness and the erratic or rude comments of other people, we loved the freedom of relying on God for the best timing of babies. But there were also other pivotal events happening around this time in the life of our family. God was providing plenty of opportunities for us to learn to trust Him for all our needs, not just the timing of our children.

The first of these events involved schooling. I had attended a homeschool conference during the summer, and even though I liked the idea of teaching at home, I had mentally crossed it off the list of possibilities. With so many young children, I thought it would be unrealistic to tackle such a long-term, seemingly impossible project.

Philip turned five a couple of months after Ruth came home, and he would need to begin kindergarten in the fall. My parents had offered to pay for him to attend a nearby Christian school, which seemed like a wonderful provision until we realized that Philip already knew most of what would be taught there that year. Plus, the afternoon pick-up time fell in the middle of naptime. It didn't take this already-stretched-too-thin mom long to do the math. Twice-daily car seat wrestling matches + cranky, nap-deprived kids = instant headache. I pulled out the information and catalogs I had tucked away from the conference and began educating myself on homeschooling as an option.

Our decision to educate Philip at home that year was primarily a matter of logistics. It simply felt easier and more rational to dive into homeschooling than to jump through the hoops required to send him off for a half-day program. We hoped that this option would save my sanity (along with the kids' sleep schedule), and we knew we could always choose something different the next year. I have no doubt that God used the obvious circumstances to push us in that direction. It was a determination born of desperation, but it still required a step of faith.

We lurched and hobbled through that first year, trying to figure out what worked, learning to maneuver through the constant interruptions inherent with four younger children (Samuel was born in October). Some days we wanted to quit.

Other days we loved it, but either way, we continued to press on. When the next year arrived, we resumed teaching and never looked back. Homeschooling was the educational option that best fit our family.

In addition to the schooling issue, God also stretched us in the area of finances. After Ruth came home, we didn't have a vehicle large enough to transport our family of six so we bought an old van with the little bit of money we had left. One of our two cars then became an "extra" vehicle which we loaned to the church for a single mom to use.

Brad drove our twelve-year-old Chevette hatchback to and from his paper sales job and for an occasional delivery. The plan was to drive that until it died, then transition to the small sedan which was a few years newer. Even though it was our best and newest vehicle, the car had seen its better days. It bore numerous scratches from the steel wool I zealously used as a young bride to remove patches of tree sap and sported the hailstorm pock marks we never fixed because we used the insurance money for a down payment on our house. The car also boasted some age-related mechanical quirks, but it could generally be depended on to move people from one location to another. We were happy for someone else to use it until we needed it.

Several weeks after we dropped off the "loaner" vehicle at church, a woman from the benevolence committee surprised me with a call. I stretched the extra-long phone cord as far away from the noise of the children as I could, straining to hear what she had to say.

Cherry didn't waste any time getting to her point. "I really think God is up to something here. Would you be willing to *give* your car to the lady using it rather than *loaning* it?"

Caught off guard by her request, my immediate response was: *But we are going to need that car.* As soon as the thought popped into my head, God planted a sure reality in the soil of my dismay. **Don't *I* meet all your needs?** *Yes, Lord. It's not the car. It's You.*

There's just no arguing with a reminder like that. Brad agreed and with that clear and generous reassurance from God, we joyfully let the car go. As it turned out, a few years later when we did need another vehicle, God provided a fifteen-passenger van. He knew that we would end up with fourteen people in our family and our five-passenger car would've been about as helpful as using a motorcycle for a school bus. I'm so glad we didn't self-ishly attempt to hold onto something ridiculously inadequate out of fear that God wouldn't come through.

In addition to vehicle growing pains, we started dreaming of a little more living space. Our just-under-1500-square-foot house had a huge, attached four-car garage used by the previous owner as a workshop. The potential to expand into that space was one thing that had drawn us to the house, and we wanted to explore dropping a wall in the garage to extend our living area. We also hoped for a third bathroom. Around the time of Ruth's last surgery, we approached a contractor in our Sunday school class about giving us an estimate. We planned to attempt some of the work ourselves and use Charlie's skill where needed. Looking back, that was laughably unrealistic since we had no building know-how and no YouTube to consult.

But God provided despite our lack of competence, and He orchestrated a volunteer force out of our Sunday school class, graciously headed by Charlie. Willing workers descended upon our house at odd times—sometimes one or two, sometimes a big group—to help with our garage addition. They dropped a wall, added a big window, plumbed in a bathroom, and helped with heat and air.

By the end of the project, we had about six hundred additional square feet of living space and could still park two cars in the garage that was left. At first, we used the area as a guest room and homeschool space. Eventually adding three bunkbeds gave six little heads a place to rest. Having that third bathroom was crucial too. It was an amazing provision long before we realized how much we would need it.

Hebrews 11:6 informs us that "without faith it is impossible to please Him, for he who comes to God must believe that He is, and that He is a rewarder of those who seek Him." Following Jesus requires faith—sometimes big leaps and sometimes small, daily steps, but always moving toward the Lord and His Word despite what our sight, feelings, or the culture around us says makes sense. Choosing to act by faith will be necessary throughout our lives, and it won't necessarily get easier as we go. But when we move in faith, we can be confident that we will always find the treasure of Jesus on the other side.

For Brad and me, adopting Ruth, beginning to homeschool, and pressing into the Lord's heart for life by trusting Him with the timing and number of children He wanted to give us were significant steps of faith that solidified an acceptance of God's calling and provision for our family and laid a foundation for years to come. Jesus was inviting us into a beautiful heritage—a surprising adventure of faith and dependence on Him.

Out of Control

EMBRACING THE BEAUTY OF REST

And He said, "My presence shall go with
you, and I will give you rest."
Exodus 33:14

We were now thoroughly in the thick of things. Our first year of homeschooling was in the books, Brad was working hard in his sales position, and I was navigating the daily dance of life with littles. Right after Samuel's first birthday, my cycles resumed and our sixth child was on his way.

By this time, we had become a curiosity wherever we went. People often gawked as Brad and I shepherded our growing family through shopping center parking lots or down grocery store aisles. At first, these astonished observers would ask if we ran a daycare; then, realizing all the children were ours, their next question was often, "Are you Catholic?" "Mormon?" "Crazy?" No one actually articulated the crazy part, but their tone of voice often implied it.

There were also constant comments about how we took care of all of them. "I can't handle the two I have. How do you manage with six [or eight or however many we had at the time]?"

I didn't realize how often we were cornered with these comments until one day an older gentleman stopped us in the grocery store parking lot, politely curious about our family size. The kids wiggled and hopped, energy bursting from every joint while I attempted to contain their enthusiasm long enough to answer his questions. After a moment of chitchat, he crouched to Philip's eye level and asked, "Are you going to have a big family when you grow up, young man?"

Philip paused his game of "don't step on the cracks or you'll break your mother's back" and hesitated for a moment, his blue eyes fixed earnestly on the man's face. "I don't know," he replied. "I'm not sure I could handle that many." Only six years old at the time, he parroted the words he had heard so often about our family.

Of course, these astonished strangers had a point. Mothering that many young children was a challenge, and even simple errands like going to the grocery store often turned into a major undertaking. But God was continuing to grow us along with our children, and though our lives were often hectic, there was a little more method to the madness. We were beginning to develop rhythms that would be essential to our family's well-being, and we were learning the scriptural and sacred value of rest.

ANOTHER DAY IN PARADISE

My day usually began early in the morning—often after nursing an infant in the wee hours of the night. I would attempt to wake before the masses and spend a couple of quiet moments with the Lord. As every mother can attest, no matter how early you try to rise to accomplish something, the baby or toddler somehow knows that Mom is up. And once Mom is up, the party has started. I don't know how many times I reminded the Lord during those years that if He would just allow the baby to snooze a little longer, I might actually be able to read my Bible.

Naturally, once the baby was up the rest of the world was eager to join the fun. And then there was no looking back. Diaper changes preceded the breakfast scramble which included the distribution of a couple of menu items accompanied by a nursing session or spoon feeding. After a haphazard cleanup, we dove into teeth brushing, attempts at the potty, and chores before settling down to snuggle with a book and begin school. Special toys used only during school time distracted active toddlers for five minutes or so—on a good day. Then my time was divided between the math lesson and the constant interruptions. Sitting still on the couch for two short minutes made this up-several-times-in-the-night mama just plain drowsy. I've often joked that I taught each one of our children to read while snoozing. I took turns with one of the older ones on his schoolwork while another older child helped play with the younger ones until his turn at the books.

Later in the morning, we usually tried to go outside for a bit of fresh air and a change of pace, as well as an opportunity to run off some energy. Sometimes we would load up a double stroller and take a walk or blow bubbles in the front yard. Lunch at our house came early—11:00 a.m. Peanut butter and jelly sandwiches were the usual fare unless we were fortunate enough to have some leftovers from the evening before.

After lunch, we straightened up a bit and then settled down to read together. Naps arrived promptly at one, followed by free time and prep for supper. We usually ate just after five as Dad walked in the door. Then playtime began in earnest. Dad was always the fun one. Seven thirty ushered in snacks and the kids' target bedtime was nine. By then I was usually ready to head to bed too.

That was our loose schedule. It gave our days a flexible structure even if things came up and the times weren't exact. The kids and I basically knew what was coming next and that gave us stability. Of course, at times we played at the park, had an appointment, or invited friends over and abandoned the schedule, but we always had an idea of what needed to happen next to get back on track and finish out the day with some kind of order. The predictable rhythm of mealtimes, schooltime, and naptime gave our long days a needed organization and familiarity.

After our adoption of Ruth and the birth of Samuel, the babies came in a pleasantly predictable pattern over the next five and a half years. Josiah, our sixth child, arrived in July 1998. Simeon made his debut in March 2000. Lydia bounced into the family in February 2002. And Hannah arrived the day after Christmas 2003. That made babies six through nine—all less than two years apart.

Each time a child was born, we worked hard to get the new baby on our family schedule as soon as possible. Of course, extra naps and feeding times were required, but we worked to make sure that many of these activities overlapped. Keeping the entire family on a schedule helped my sanity as a mom.

GOODBYE, PERFECTIONISM

During these busy years, my emotions often fluctuated from day to day and even several times a day. One moment I would be so thankful to be home with these little people I loved more than life itself. The next I would be wringing my hands about how I'd already ruined Philip and wondering if there was any hope I'd do better with the other children. And this was a job I cherished. I wanted to be home. I wanted to homeschool my children. I wanted to add more babies and be the major influence in their young lives. But that didn't mean it was easy.

Whenever I started feeling like my life was one huge vortex of exhaustion and endless demands, I acknowledged my feelings of desperation and then did my best to simply sleep. My perspective always leaned toward overload when I was extra tired. Counseling might have helped, and certainly an extended and leisurely trip to the beach would have been excellent therapy (in my opinion), but neither was a realistic possibility for me. A shower and a nap often proved my best options, and usually after a day or so, I was ready to hit the ground running with a much-refreshed attitude. I didn't have time to get sucked into a pity party, so instead I indulged in a pity moment, then tried to rest before jumping back into the fray. Somehow the Lord preserved my health and my sanity during those hectic years. Whenever I was at the end of my own strength, He generously supplied the vision and the energy I needed to keep going.

In addition to not taking my whining and overwhelm too seriously, I finally decided perfectionism wasn't welcome in our home and I shoved it out the door. It's downright difficult to stay on top of everything when you have several children whose ages all begin and end with a single digit. The house is going to be messy, the children are going to fuss, and sometimes Mom is going to feel frazzled. The jig is up. No more pretending to myself or others that I have this thing all figured out and under control. I no longer had the time or the energy to play that game. I often joked that it took a lot for God to finally convince me to shed my perfectionistic tendencies. **Oh, so you want things to function flawlessly? Here, have a baby. Still feeling like you have all this under control? Here's another one. Still? Again? Not cured yet? Have another and another and another.**

God obviously has a keen sense of humor. And I finally took the lesson to heart.

KEEPING IT REAL

So how did we handle the practical realities that allowed us to function each day? What did that look like at our house? "Clean" usually meant toys were picked up, and on a good day, one of the kids had run the vacuum across the rug. We made sure the dishes were washed and the kitchen useable, but the kids' rooms rarely got attention. In general, if you got an item out you were supposed to put it back and maybe even leave the area a little nicer than you found it. At least in theory. On tougher days, just shoveling a trail to walk through the toys was all we managed.

The level of disarray might not make sense for empty nesters or a young married couple without children. There were lots of times I wished my environment was more organized (and actually cleaned), but in general, with a couple of straightening efforts a day, we could function and keep the living areas livable. We didn't have a perfect system, but in the house of a large family, it worked pretty well. We let good enough be good enough.

Not surprisingly, meeting the constant needs of so many little ones, endeavoring to educate the school-aged children, and attempting to keep a household running reasonably well invited overwhelm to visit often—even without the disapproving taskmaster of perfectionism.

One day, shortly after the birth of Josiah, was particularly difficult. I woke to his cry much earlier than normal. I had been up several times in the night—nursing and also comforting Samuel, who wasn't feeling well. I stumbled over blocks, wooden puzzle pieces, and board books. Everything my tired eyes took in demoralized me. I fed Josiah, then faced the fact that falling back into bed just wasn't an option. Ten minutes later, the troops rallied in earnest. I sluggishly trudged through the motions of changing diapers and preparing breakfast. Two milk spills and a temper tantrum accompanied our morning meal, but eventually, breakfast was over and we gathered to begin our schoolwork.

I tried to work on reading with Isaac while I held Josiah fussing in my lap. Abigail and Ruth started arguing over a toy and Samuel toddled off to create mischief in a more secluded spot. By the time Isaac and I encountered our fifth interruption, we were both frustrated. Abigail was crying because Ruth had hit her and Ruth was crying because Abigail had won the toy tug-of-war. Samuel decided he was hungry again and Philip used the general chaos as an opportunity to leave his math assignment and start building an edifice with wooden blocks—which Samuel promptly knocked over. Philip's reaction suggested it was a tragedy equal to the fall of Rome.

I spoke sharply to everyone and no one in particular. "For crying out loud, what is going on?!" I rolled my eyes and gathered everyone in the middle of the living room floor. It was time for a reset. A toddler-sized motivational talk and a quick game helped everyone's attitude—including my own. Then it was time to try again. I wish I could say that was a rare occurrence, but any mom knows chaos happens with surprising regularity.

It would have been nice for my children to always be well-behaved and kind toward each other. I would have preferred a spill- and tantrum-free day. Babies sleeping through the night immediately after birth, never-sick toddlers, and school sessions with eager, attentive students would top my list of a mom's dream come true. But our house didn't function like that. Attaining some picturesque ideal was beyond my control, but what I could control was telling myself the truth. God was helping me mother my children. He was growing my patience and wisdom. These moments were to be cherished; they would not last. And even the most mundane, repetitive tasks were pleasing to the Lord as I served Him, my husband, and my children.

Propping up our day with the scaffolding of a predictable schedule, ditching perfectionism, and replacing my whining with the truth were three practical ways to manage during this time, but these strategies alone were incomplete. What I desperately needed in order to thrive in my role as a mother, was rest.

THE GIFT OF SABBATH

Rest can seem impossibly elusive to a mom. Even during a long-anticipated family vacation, the children still need to be fed and messes still require cleaning. A mom's work is literally never done. We are always "on-call." But that doesn't mean we never get to rest.

I'm not talking about the temporary, surface distraction of a TV-watching binge, although I can occasionally appreciate the predictably happy ending of a Hallmark movie. What we need is deep, restorative, replenishing rest—a time to recover and regroup, not merely "escape." God created us with that need, wiring it deep within our bodies and souls.

And He also made provision for that need. The Lord instituted rest at the very beginning: "By the seventh day God completed His work which He had done, and He rested on the seventh day from all His work which He had done. Then God blessed the seventh day and sanctified it, because in it He rested from all His work which God had created and made" (Genesis 2:2–3).

God rested by example and then gave His people a day of rest, the Sabbath, as a gift. Observing the Sabbath was an act of faith and obedience for His people then, and it remains an act of faith and obedience for us today. God commanded it and sustained His people as they set aside one day a week for a special time of rest and worship. The Sabbath reminds us of Who our provider is and helps us to recognize our physical limitations. It provides a reset for our bodies and our spirits as we look to the Lord for all our needs—physical, emotional, and spiritual.

I admit that the Sabbath is a gift I'm still learning how to enjoy. Moms typically can't take a whole day off every week, especially when they have young children. Still, we can incorporate a more slow-paced schedule, make meals ahead that can be easily heated, do a little extra the evening before so the house is picked up, and choose to focus on the Lord in a special way as a family. The Sabbath isn't meant to restrict us or give us one more thing to accomplish on our list. It is an invitation to recover and reconnect with God. We can anticipate the Sabbath as a merciful part of our beautiful heritage.

RECOGNIZING THE SEASON

In addition to incorporating Sabbath rest into our week, we can also build restful habits into our day-to-day rhythms. Recognizing and cooperating with our current season is one way to practice moving toward rest in freedom and expectation rather than under stress and obligation.

In the life of any family, some seasons are more opportune than others for tackling a project or accomplishing a big goal. Rhythms and routines that make sense in one year (or even in one quarter) must be adjusted in the next to accommodate a constantly changing reality. Family life is fluid, and simply acknowledging and cooperating with our current circumstances goes a long way toward eliminating unnecessary friction and frustration. For instance, every other year during the weeks of pregnancy sickness, we didn't attempt to accomplish a lot of school—even if it wasn't summer break. The older children who could read still worked and they helped the younger ones with simple math or learning the alphabet. But I didn't expect a lot of progress. Attempting to maintain our normal school schedule during those early weeks of pregnancy would have produced exasperation and disappointment in all of us. We simply adjusted to the temporary situation and picked up the slack later.

On the other hand, after the birth of a baby, we were able to press into school a little more. We were home a lot and there was always a book handy when I sat down to nurse. No longer dealing with the constant nausea made all the difference in my energy levels and our school progress.

Just knowing how these rhythms worked for us kept me from panicking in the stages that were less productive and encouraged me to take advantage of opportunity when life was more accommodating.

Another way we acknowledged the reality of our situation centered around sports and extra-curricular activities. Even if every child only played one sport, we would've been crushed by impossible time demands. And dragging toddlers around to multiple games a week wasn't our idea of fun. We decided (after a couple of stints with Little League and peewee soccer) that the sports world could survive just fine without us. That family philosophy was one we expanded to other areas in life, too. In general, we did our best to bundle our minimal time and energy with multiple children participating in the same activity—or waiting until a child really showed interest and commitment to pursue a passion.

Don't get me wrong. The kids did participate in outside activities, including some sports. But since we guarded against a blanket assumption that they had to be involved in multiple childhood pursuits, we were able to spread our activities out in such a way that our family life as a whole didn't suffer.

Philip loved chess and became quite good at it—winning the state scholastic championship twice during his high school years. My parents were able to take him to some out-of-town chess tournaments and a couple of the other siblings tagged along and enjoyed the game too. Isaac and Abigail started piano lessons with a woman who agreed to teach at our house, and then several of the younger ones began playing and Isaac also took up the violin. Eventually, Lydia and Hannah played volleyball with a league at the YMCA. The kids were also involved with church activities. In general, low-key commitments, overlapping commitments, and the decision not to juggle too many commitments at once rescued us from being constantly gone from home. Even without a big family some of these ideas can help serve as a buffer from the busyness and overwhelm so common in our culture today.

MOW THERAPY

The breeze cooled my sun-warmed skin on a beautiful spring afternoon. It was naptime, but instead of sleeping, I had picked up a couple of stray toys and a piece of trash in the yard, then retrieved the mower out of the garage. Three pushes on the flexible red fuel button, a squeeze of the handle, and a firm tug on the pull cord made the engine roar to life. I lined the wheels up with the edge of the street and began the trek across our lawn.

Mowing wasn't my job, and it seems counterintuitive that I would add any kind of work to my already stuffed schedule, but to me, an occasional grass-cutting session was surprisingly therapeutic.

I breathed in the fresh air and the onion-tinged scent of the cut grass. As I pushed the mower back and forth across the front lawn, the high weeds succumbed to the blade and lay short and neat behind me. The yard provided visual confirmation of my progress one glorious row at a time. I could see and measure my accomplishment with each new strip of neatly-trimmed grass. And unlike almost every other area of my life, no one could come along and mess up what I had just achieved.

In so much of a mom's domain, we don't see progress. Growth is slow. The shaping of a child's heart toward maturity and responsibility is almost imperceptible in each day's training and correction. Even tasks that show promise of completion are undone too quickly to feel much accomplishment. Meals are eaten in a matter of minutes. Laundry washed, folded, and put away is mysteriously replaced with more dirty piles than seems humanly possible. And a tidied-up room is easily (and quickly) demolished by a couple of exuberant toddlers. But mowing holds a rare permanency. My efforts would last a whole week before needing to be repeated! In my world of almost constant re-doing, that felt amazing.

For me, mowing provides a sense of achievement and durability that lifts my spirits, a few moments to let my mind rest or ponder something important, and the physical and calming benefits of exercise and time out of doors. No wonder that little red machine and I are good friends. And since mowing isn't my job, I can quit anytime I want and I still get brownie points for helping with the lawn. Win, win, win, and win again!

If mowing sounds more like drudgery than delight, there are plenty of other possibilities for a calming, replenishing activity. Taking a hot bath, grabbing coffee with a friend, organizing a messy pantry, reading a book, going on a hike, or doing something creative comes to mind. The aforementioned beach escape with long walks and a good book would be ideal (but again, not usually realistic). There are as many ideas of what would be relaxing as there are mamas who could use a break. The point is to know what is helpful, what is possible, and then schedule it in occasionally as a way to nourish your spirit.

OUR ONE NON-NEGOTIABLE

It may seem simplistic or unrealistic, but the institution of an established naptime worked wonders for our family. Naps in our house were non-negotiable. No matter the age, we shut things down for a couple of hours every afternoon for a time of rest and renewal. Tired, grumpy children slept and woke up refreshed. Older children weren't required to sleep, but they had to stay in their beds reading or playing quietly by themselves. It allowed them to have some time alone in our crowded household. An afternoon rest greatly benefitted me too. I occasionally worked on something I really wanted to accomplish, but most of the time, I fell into bed, slept hard, and woke ready to tackle our late afternoon and evening routine. Naptime broke up the day and was a shining oasis to look forward to on particularly chaotic mornings. I'm not exaggerating when I say I would not have survived without it.

FILLING UP WITH THE WORD

I sat in a row with three other seasoned moms looking into the faces of a couple of dozen eager young women bursting with parenting questions. We had been invited to participate in a Q and A panel during a weekend Bible retreat. It wasn't long before a petite lady with an infant on her lap and a diaper bag slung across the back of her chair spoke up. "What does your time with God look like?"

The veteran mom on my left answered first. "I find that I'm able to commune with God through nature. My heart is lifted in praise when I'm immersed in the beauty He created."

Several women in the audience nodded in agreement.

"Just do what you can and don't feel guilty about what you can't do. God understands this season of life." The cute brunette at the end of the row tucked a stray lock of hair behind her ear as she spoke.

More heads bounced up and down in response to her input.

"I try to pray often throughout the day while I'm taking care of the children," the third mom offered with a shrug. "It's hard to attempt some kind of scheduled time."

The women on the panel all answered graciously. Every mom who has tried to meet with the Lord knows it is a struggle. Often sleep-deprived and always on call, it is rare for a mom to make it through a few minutes of Bible reading or prayer without falling asleep or being interrupted. Yet I still felt compelled to offer a little more encouragement.

"These are excellent ideas and I have often benefited from meeting with God in those ways. But I want to encourage you that it is worth it to do everything possible to absorb God's Word. Don't sweat it when it doesn't work out, but keep making the effort. Nothing replaces actually being in the Word. Nothing."

When I made that statement, I was preaching to myself. I wish I had been more faithful, and more consistent with the treasure of God's Word. It gives wisdom. It changes us. It accomplishes what God desires. The Lord speaks to us in a God-revealing, life-giving, soul-searching book and that book is worth pursuing with a tenacious effort.

Today, we have technology that I couldn't even imagine then. Our phones carry apps containing the whole Bible in multiple translations. We can listen to sermons or podcasts and access Bible study tools that help us with context and the meaning of words in the original Hebrew and Greek. Moms can't claim more time than they used to, but our access to the Word has multiplied exponentially.

In the end, it doesn't matter the means. I still occasionally handwrite verses to memorize on index cards that I can carry with me. I still prefer Scripture I can hold so I can listen to the whisper of thin, precious pages and notate key truths with my blue pen. But I also take advantage of the amazing technology available on the touchscreen I carry in my pocket.

I occasionally fall asleep as I attempt to pray or read or listen to the Word. But as long as the Lord allows me the ability to pursue Him through His Word, I will keep coming back. I know He will meet me there. And He provides rest for my soul.

SHARED CELEBRATION

Our family gathered in the living room, all of us sitting on the floor or crouching on our knees in a haphazard circle. We coaxed and beckoned with outstretched arms: "Hannah, Hannah—this way!"

Our voices rose in friendly rivalry, each eager to snag Hannah's attention and favor. "No, come to me!" "This way, Hannah!"

Hannah decided on a direction and took a couple of faltering steps before falling into Simeon's arms. We all clapped and whooped and hollered while Sim turned her around and helped her regain her balance. Hannah grinned with delight, looking from face to face before once again toddling toward a welcoming pair of arms.

We stayed in our circle until her unsteady legs grew tired, and then we gave Hannah a final cheer as Brad scooped her up into a bear hug. She was learning to walk—and we all shared in the excitement.

That scenario played out at least once with each child in our family. It was never planned, but those early steps always drew us into a laughing, cheering romp. At first, it was just Brad and me on either side trying to persuade Philip forward. But our circle grew as our family grew, and no one wanted to miss out.

Gathering around each child as they learned to walk is a perfect picture of what it means to be in a family—to love and be loved and to celebrate each other. Each person in the circle left what they had been doing to cheer on Hannah's efforts because learning a new skill is something worth being acknowledged—and each one of us was there to cheer her on. It was evident on Hannah's face that she delighted in the attention and was proud of her new accomplishment; sometimes she would pivot, either from unsteadiness or a mischievous desire to make her way toward a different admirer. This was her moment and she knew we were all thrilled for her.

When we celebrate a specific family member, we are showing appreciation and love for that person in a way that builds them up. When we celebrate the Lord's faithfulness, we acknowledge His character and offer our worship. These kinds of celebrations invite us to turn aside from the busyness of our day and savor what is in front of us.

God is the One Who originally invited us to temporarily turn aside from our ordinary occupations to focus on celebration. The Lord mandated several feasts each calendar year for His people to remind them of His past faithfulness, point to the coming Messiah, and provide an opportunity for worship and rest.

We have similar traditions. Our holidays call for feasting and special acknowledgment of God's blessings, including Jesus's birth at Christmas and His resurrection at Easter. Birthdays, anniversaries, graduations, and special accomplishments are all easy to commemorate and usually have built-in tributes. But even the simple joys of ordinary days can be noted in meaningful ways.

Pausing to give thanks as a family or enjoy a sunset together provides a welcome moment of relaxation during an otherwise full day. One area in the house clear of clutter and adorned with a bouquet of fresh flowers is a spot of beauty that gives our eyes and our minds a respite. Taking the time to notice and participate in what a child is delighting in or in a moment of shared laughter provides a special refreshment. It doesn't have to be elaborate; simply being present to the glimpses of everyday wonder and beauty around us helps to restore our souls.

Choosing to celebrate together, choosing to make things special in the midst of ordinary life is a significant kind of rest. It is the rest of a shared, beautiful history with family members and with the Lord. We all need simple celebration—pausing to mark our blessings, acknowledge beauty, and honor the Giver.

TRUE REST

All of the suggestions mentioned above are a means to rest. Schedules build habits that allow us to move forward without making the same tedious decisions every day. Cooperating with our season of life allows us to make progress without fighting against the constraints of our current circumstances. Physical rest and restorative activities give us the energy to persevere. Celebration acknowledges the beautiful and hopeful things in life, and feasting on the Word provides wisdom and refreshment as we remind ourselves of the truth of God's character and His great love for us.

These are worthwhile practices to build into our lives because rest is important. But Jesus is our ultimate source of rest. The gospels tell us that Jesus is Lord of the Sabbath (Mark 2:28). In Matthew 11:28, Jesus offers this invitation: "Come to Me, all who are weary and heavy-laden, and I will give you rest." Of course, there are rich theological implications embedded here, including the good news that Jesus is our righteousness. We are free from the impossible pursuit of earning our salvation. We can rest in His finished work on our behalf.

This is also a powerful invitation that has wide appeal for worn-out mamas. Since Jesus is our rest and our righteousness, it doesn't all depend upon us. We don't have to panic over our mistakes or our kids' mistakes. We don't have to fall apart when we don't have all the answers. We can trust God in the process. Although it might not seem possible, the Lord loves our children even more than we do and He can reach their hearts even when we feel like our efforts are failing. As moms, we don't have to be perfect or even "enough" for our children, because Jesus is our sufficiency. He is our source of truth, strength, and hope, and we can rest and rejoice in Him, knowing we are not alone in this task of shepherding our families.

ORDINARY FAITHFULNESS

Mothering multiple children of any age is a challenge. In the thick of things, life can feel chaotic and out of control. But as I navigated these difficult years, I grew more and more content and at ease. My circumstances hadn't changed, but God was changing *me*. I could finally relax in my relationship with the Lord—no longer fearing His displeasure at every turn. I was also enjoying my children without the constant worry of what I was doing wrong to ruin them.

I didn't have all the answers, but a few years of walking with the Lord and seeing His faithfulness and direction in our home-schooling and our parenting gave me confidence as I mothered. I had reached my late thirties and mellowed a lot. Brad and I made a great team, and in general, we were content and satisfied with our life. There was always lots of chaos and messes, but also lots of fun and laughter and working and playing together. It was a sweet spot.

There wasn't some huge leap of faith that God required during these years. Instead, we learned the rhythm of being faithful in the small and ordinary. We worked together where God had placed us and experienced His joy in everyday tasks and circumstances. As we moved forward step by step, we learned to rest in the beautiful heritage God was building for us and for our family.

The Shadow of Death

EMBRACING THE BEAUTY OF LOSS

*The LORD is near to the brokenhearted and
saves those who are crushed in spirit.*
Psalm 34:18

Things were finally quiet in the back of our fifteen-passenger van. The older kids were reading or listening to music with headphones. The younger ones, including Hannah, had all succumbed to sleep thanks to the lulling motion of interstate driving. We were on the way to Granddaddy and Grandmommie's house in Kentucky. I shifted in my seat and reached into my bag to retrieve the slender, plastic test stick. I looked at the double-lined result window and smiled at Brad, content and drowsy as a cat sitting in the sun puddle warming my seat. I had taken the test that morning and confirmed that baby number ten was on her way—right on time. Everything felt right in our world.

We settled in at my grandparents' house with a flurry of hugs and bringing in bags and stretching tired legs from the three-hour ride. The usual fun and antics followed, and finally, at the close of the evening, we had everyone tucked in snugly to sleep.

That's when I realized I was spotting.

Shock immobilized me for several seconds before I could compose myself enough to begin pleading to the Lord for the life of our baby. I had never spotted before during pregnancy, so even a small amount of bleeding alarmed me. As I drew a shaky breath, I attempted to reassure myself. A few of my friends had spotted while pregnant, and their babies were born strong and healthy. But that was not my normal.

All during the long night I prayed and dozed, dozed and prayed, but the spotting continued. The next day, Brad and I anxiously implored the Lord to protect our little one. We drove home Sunday afternoon, and late that evening, the spotting transitioned into a heavier flow. My shock transitioned into full-blown panic. Had the Lord given and taken away?

Monday arrived to offer some relief and hope. For fifteen hours, I stopped bleeding completely. I dared to believe that the worst was over and was relieved to see a beautiful positive result Tuesday morning when I took another test. But the spotting soon began again.

In the months leading up to this moment, I had attempted to wake each morning before the rest of the house stirred. Tiptoeing into the living room, I would turn on the antique brass lamp and settle on the couch. Then I would open my worn Bible to the Psalms and copy verse after verse into my spiral-bound journal— anything that was at all applicable to my life or pointed out God's character. I began with Psalm 1, sometimes writing the entire chapter, sometimes skipping a section here and there, but building my own personal praise and prayer book one stanza at a time. And God was building in me a calm assurance of His kindness and care, and an increased awareness of His glory. I'm not sure what prompted me to begin that process; I simply felt an invitation to camp out with the Lord in this much beloved book filled with the highs and lows of human emotion—often beginning with despair or fear, and eventually fighting through to praise, as God's faithfulness was called to mind.

Each morning, I was exposed to the language of lament, praise, surrender, sorrow, and joy. It was all fresh and at my fingertips. And though I hadn't realized it then, those hours spent in the Psalms were preparing me for the distress I was encountering now, as I faced the possibility of losing a child.

As alternating waves of hope and fear swelled around me, I headed to the Psalms to calm my heart. "When my anxious thoughts multiply within me, Your consolations delight my soul" (Psalm 94:19). I skipped around, finding verses I had previously underlined, and prayed them back to my Father. *God, You know I am anxious. I need Your consolation.* "For the Lord God is a sun and shield; the Lord gives grace and glory; no good thing does He withhold from those who walk uprightly" (Psalm 84:11). *Lord, please be a shield to our baby. Give us grace and glory. We know that whatever is good, You will not withhold.* After a few minutes of the Word's reinforcement, my ever-present panic settled into a quieter apprehension.

On Wednesday morning, my midwife gently informed me that she thought I had expelled the baby Sunday evening when my bleeding was heavier. She ordered bloodwork to check my progesterone and hCG levels, but sent me home with little hope.

That evening I shut myself up in the bedroom after tucking the younger ones in bed. Continuing my constant plea for life, I flipped to the Psalms again, searching for reassurance and comfort. "Blessed be the Lord, who daily bears our burden, the God who is our salvation. God is to us a God of deliverances; and to God the Lord belong escapes from death" (Psalm 68:19–20). *Father, to You belong escapes from death. You are able to protect our baby. Please, please spare this child.*

A single tear softly plinked on the page, leaving a smear as I brushed it away. I rubbed my eyes and continued reading in the next chapter—this time methodically searching instead of frantically jumping here and there.

"But I am afflicted and in pain; may your salvation, O God,

set me securely on high. I will praise the name of God with song, and shall magnify Him with thanksgiving. And it will please the Lord better than an ox" (Psalm 69:29–31). These verses brought me to a fast stop—they seemed to describe me perfectly. I was afflicted and in pain. Could even my feeble praise and thanksgiving during this time really please the Lord more than sacrifice? I bit my bottom lip and managed a slight smile.

I *was* thankful. This child was a gift… no matter what happened. She was planned and formed by her Creator and given to us. That admission released a steady gratefulness greater than my fear and pain. It permeated my weary heart and overflowed in praise. I sat quietly before the Lord for a while with my eyes closed and my open hands resting on my Bible.

I still didn't know the outcome of this pregnancy, but I clung to hope. Maybe the Lord would even yet spare our baby. Regardless, at this moment of quiet surrender, I brought Him delight. In the midst of my aching, this realization produced a sweet joy. The awareness of the Lord's presence and the joy that had taken root sustained me for the next several hours of uncertainty.

By the next morning, the uncertainty was over. I had miscarried. Later in the day, my bloodwork results also confirmed our sorrow. Our child was gone.

GOD CHOOSES

Miscarriage. It was something I had dreaded and feared for as long as I understood what it was. I desired children. I delighted in children. I celebrated life. I didn't want any part of this sorrow. But I was informed that from a medical perspective, I could likely expect more of the same.

Older moms have older eggs and often those eggs are no longer strong and healthy. Statistically, women in their late thirties and early forties are more likely to miscarry and less likely to conceive.[1] Mere days from my thirty-ninth birthday, I was living proof of that reality.

The statistics are discouraging, and the likelihood of further miscarriage gave me pause. But what I clung to as I pondered my loss is that God is bigger than any statistic. Old eggs and bad odds both bow to His command. I knew the Lord often works within scientific and medical probabilities—there is a season of fertility that eventually wanes—but by now I was so convinced of the Lord's sovereignty that I didn't dwell there. I was only 39, and my age was not some insurmountable obstacle preventing God from giving us more children if He desired. And we could still ask Him for that blessing, regardless of how He might choose to answer.

GRIEVING WITH HOPE

God makes it clear in His Word that He values life. He is the One Who authors it (Acts 17:25) and He is the One Who ordains our days before any of them come to pass (Psalm 139:16). Of course, the Lord is not confined to our limited view of time. He is the master of immortality. Each conception He orchestrates launches a soul into eternity. No matter how short our time to enjoy a beloved child here on earth, our child still exists. Even though it is excruciating, miscarriage doesn't negate the preciousness of the gift or the honor bestowed. A mom who has experienced a miscarriage is still a mother. The child lost-too-soon is a delight to the Lord and is delighting in the Lord's presence. God is invested in the long story.

I didn't know how to reconcile all this in my mind and heart, but I took some consolation in knowing I had been chosen for the privilege of mothering this child, even if only for mere days. My body nurtured a beloved eternal soul briefly before she entered the Lord's presence.

All this was a comfort to me, but we still had to trudge

through the heartache. There is never a clear roadmap through grief, but we took some tentative steps as a family. We decided to write a note to our baby (or draw a picture, if that was more age appropriate). We compiled these messages and remembrances in a baby book of sorts—a scrapbook dedicated to our child. Something about writing down our thoughts and sorrows was comforting. The scrapbook gave us a physical object we could see and touch, a tangible reminder of this baby.

In so many ways, the pain of miscarriage hides in obscurity. There is no funeral, no public acknowledgment of a precious life lost, no standard or formal way to honor a cherished child and bring some means of closure. Often parents and families grieve quietly, without recognition or support.

But when we have Jesus, we do not grieve alone. Our Savior was "a man of sorrows and acquainted with grief" (Isaiah 53:3). Jesus knows what it is like to hurt. He knows what it is like to mourn. And He knows how to "comfort us in all our afflictions" (2 Corinthians 1:4).

I did experience the Lord's comfort. He met me in His Word and ministered to me again and again as I sought Him in my sorrow. And He did the same for Brad.

NO REGRETS

I walked down the nursery hallway at church. The corridor was comfortably crowded with parents and their offspring bumping gently through the Sunday morning drop-off and pick-up pipeline. I stopped and turned when I felt a hand on my shoulder.

I recognized the curly red-headed young woman, but I didn't recall her name.

"Congratulations!" she exclaimed with a broad smile. She was obviously pregnant herself and warmly welcoming me back into the shared bond of expectant motherhood.

Tears sprang to my eyes, but I answered evenly. "Thank you, but we lost the baby."

She flushed and faltered a bit. "I'm so sorry. I...I didn't mean to..."

I interrupted her with a touch on her arm. "It's really ok. You couldn't have known. And thank you for being excited for us."

She nodded, gave me a quick hug, and scurried away.

I felt bad for her and honestly a little bad for me, too.

We could have avoided that scene, of course. We understood the caution some couples exercise to keep their "we're expecting" news close until after the first trimester when miscarriage is less likely. It's not easy to be congratulated when everything you see is colored with grief. In a lot of ways, it makes sense to wait.

But Brad and I typically told the children immediately— usually the same day we had the proof of a positive pregnancy test. We were so excited, and they were too. They loved to share baby news with friends and acquaintances from church. It was so much a part of their joy that we never restrained their enthusiasm. And by this time, with nine children, anyone who knew us pretty much expected our announcements.

This baby was no exception. We had been quick to share our joy, but we waited until we were sure before explaining the miscarriage. Naturally, word of our loss didn't spread as rapidly as our pregnancy announcement had, so we faced congratulations for weeks after the miscarriage. That was distressing and difficult to field, but we didn't regret making our news known. For us, the importance of the acknowledgement and celebration of life trumped the social discomfort and personal pain of having to reveal that we were no longer expecting.

Every life is worth celebrating. It was right to acknowledge the value of this precious child. If we had waited for a later announcement, we would have lost the opportunity to freely rejoice without the burden of grief eclipsing our commemoration of life. Even though our celebration was short before the sorrow moved in, it was fitting and good that we celebrated.

As we grieved together as a family, Brad and I wanted our children to realize that they had another sweet sibling and would be able to rejoice with their brother or sister in heaven. This is not our final home and we have loved ones who have left this world before us. It was not an easy conversation, but a worthwhile one, and by this time we had some older children who could understand.

Even though sharing our "expecting" status had made the pain of loss seem sharper, it had also made our celebration sweeter. We didn't regret telling early.

HERE WE GO AGAIN

In the weeks following our loss, we kept moving forward each day, dealing with the grief as it came. Just as I was reconciling myself to what had happened and was beginning to hope for another pregnancy, I realized I was expecting again. But I was bleeding too. This time there was no doubt I was miscarrying. The realization of pregnancy and the reality of miscarriage were simultaneous.

Even though I yearned to celebrate this new life, the fresh grief swallowed up my final reserves of emotional energy. It was the only time we didn't announce a pregnancy to the kids. I simply couldn't face the heaviness of another acknowledgment, more explanation, or even the keepsake practices that had felt so helpful the last time.

This child was just as loved and wanted. This child was just as precious. But there had been no time between finding out about the baby and realizing our loss. My capacity was at its limit. I simply bundled this new sorrow into the same package occupied by our first miscarriage and continued mourning without extra fanfare. That was all I could manage.

I'm not sure what to say, God, except You know. You know what is best. You know what You are doing through all of this. You know we trust You even though we are hurting. And You know the name of our two precious children.

I was stunned by this second miscarriage and I dreaded the possibility of more. Wrapped up in my grief was also the desire—almost the demand—for reassurance that the Lord would give us more children. I didn't want to face this kind of loss again. I wanted a guarantee. However, God doesn't typically offer such an assurance, and He didn't in this instance. What He did offer was continuing comfort as we grieved, along with the assurance of His constant presence. I tried my best to decide that was enough.

But what I really wanted was to hold our babies.

Our losses encouraged me to evaluate my heart and motives. Did I long for the Lord as much as I longed for a child? Did I press into God because of His worthiness or because I wanted Him to grant my desires? I couldn't readily answer these questions and I was afraid of what that revealed about my heart. Still, I sought the Lord—haltingly and uncertainly—as I handed over my mess as best as I knew how.

I don't even know what to pray, Father, or how to pray. Please just do what is necessary. Help me to see You and trust You more.

"The Lord is near to the brokenhearted, and saves those who are crushed in spirit." (Psalm 34:18). *I am Your brokenhearted child, Father. Be near to me.*

It's in moments like these that we get to exercise truth. We get to apply what we have learned. We decide if we will call His will good, acceptable, and perfect (Romans 12:2). Will we trust Him to work things out for our ultimate good (Romans 8:28)? Will we acknowledge His goodness in the middle of our grief?

Lord, help me to cling to You and experience peace in Your decision for us—not a fearful numbness. I don't want to be reserved toward You or toward what You choose for me. I am Your daughter. May I be still in Your hand.

STILL ABUNDANCE

How can loss be a part of abundance? Of a beautiful heritage? Of the sovereign will of a good God? One answer is that loss increases our longing—for wholeness, for restoration, for Jesus. It pushes us deeper into the haven of God's comfort and causes us to cling to His peace. Loss leads us away from the trivial and highlights the eternal. It reminds us that this world is only a shadow of our true home.

Second Corinthians 4:17–18 assures us, "For momentary, light affliction is producing for us an eternal weight of glory far beyond all comparison, while we look not at the things which are seen, but at the things which are not seen; for the things which are seen are temporal, but the things which are not seen are eternal." What is right in front of us is not the end of the story. Loss isn't lasting. And all our sorrow now is nothing compared to what we will experience when everything is made right. We have hope because eventually all will be well.

Still, the affliction of miscarriage *feels* weighty. It (as well as infertility) is a tragic result of the curse earned by the fall. In Genesis 3:16, the Lord tells Eve that she will have pain in childbirth. Women who have given birth can attest to that obvious truth. Childbirth hurts. But the pain of not conceiving or of losing a child is nothing short of excruciating. It's all a part of the sorrow of living in this fallen world. And it touches some of the most tender parts of a woman's heart.

But the Lord didn't leave us with death and despair. Even before God proclaimed the curse to the man and woman, He had a plan. He addressed the serpent first and provided a way forward for His wayward people.

And I will put enmity
Between you and the woman,
And between your seed and her seed;
He shall bruise you on the head,
And you shall bruise Him on the heel. (Genesis 3:15)

This was a prophecy pointing to the Messiah. God promised to send a Savior. Redemption would rescue us, and therefore death would not be our final destiny. Jesus defeated death and reconciled us to the Father when He died on the cross and rose again.

Our heritage is secure. We belong to God's eternal family, and as His sons and daughters, we will one day be free from the curse, whole and restored in His presence.

In the meantime, we can learn from the apostle Paul's example when we face loss and adversity. We don't know the particulars of the difficulty he mentioned in 2 Corinthians 12:7–10, but Paul called it a "thorn in his flesh," and begged God three times to remove it. When the Lord denied his request, Paul learned to be content in his weakness so that he would know God's strength in a greater way.

In fact, Paul went on to embrace a willingness to lose "all things" as a means of gaining Christ—knowing Him more intimately and becoming more like Him (see Philippians 3:8–10). Paul welcomed his temporal weaknesses and losses as a means of eternal benefit. In the merciful upside-down kingdom of heaven, loss becomes gain because of the surpassing value of knowing Jesus.

Brad and I couldn't claim the same maturity as Paul, but we recognized that losing our babies in miscarriage had encouraged us to press into a deeper realization of the Lord and His power and comfort in our lives. We had begun to make the connection that loss leads to abundance because loss leads us to Jesus.

This is still abundant life. This is still mercy and kindness. This is still a beautiful heritage.

---

1. "How Aging Affects Fertility and Pregnancy." The American College of Obstetricians and Gynecologists, FAQ, October 2020, www.acog.org>women's-health/faqs/having-a-baby-after-age-35-how-aging-affects-fertility-and-pregnancy

Standing Still

EMBRACING THE BEAUTY OF WAITING

The Lord is good to those who wait for Him,
to the person who seeks Him.
Lamentations 3:25

My hands shake as I open the package. I follow the familiar instructions and hear the soft click as I lay the wand face up on the side of the sink. The countdown begins as the liquid slowly washes across the clear window. The pink control line begins to form; it's a valid test. Nothing appears on the result side, but I reassure myself that it's only been a minute and, as I learned in that pregnancy center many years ago, these things take time.

Do I see the hint of a line? A possible positive result? No, it's just wishful thinking—nothing to get excited about. Two minutes pass. The control line darkens. I stop watching for a while, praying for a distinct line the next time I look. Straightening the few things already neatly arranged on the sink top, I wait for the three-minute mark. Finally, I approach the test stick—cautiously —as if it might bite. It does; still no line. I gaze a few seconds more before grabbing the offender. Turning it this way and that, I try the light from the fixture and then the natural light flooding through the window, willing my eyes to see even the faintest of lines.

Nothing.

I chuck the wand and turn away. Later I sneak back, dig through the trash, and retrieve the stick just to make sure.

Still nothing.

STRETCHING

In the years following our decision to embrace every child God offered, life assumed a comfortable, predictable pattern. We thrived in the groove of welcoming a sweet new baby every other year in the midst of our large-family living. I approached my late thirties with no expectation of slowing down, assuming we would easily conceive and I would carry babies until closer to my mid-forties. I had always gotten pregnant quickly—usually in the first month possible—so I thought I always would. In my mind, a pregnancy in my later forties would cap things off—a glorious crowning moment before a graceful fade into menopause. I still prayed, of course, technically not taking pregnancy for granted. But I didn't realize how much I expected God to rubber-stamp my vision for what things would look like. I was rocking this mom role. There was no need for Him to rock the boat.

In fact, since my forties lurked just around the bend, I began praying that God would jump-start my cycles sooner than the customary year off after childbirth. The door would soon swing shut on my fertile years, even though at the beginning that door seemed as wide open as eternity. With this realization in mind, I longed to decrease the timeline between babies. But, as He often does when life feels predictable, God invited me to trust Him in a whole new way.

When we first put away our birth control, we felt challenged by the possibility that God might stretch us with more children than we anticipated. We never anticipated that He might stretch us by giving less. After that first miscarriage and the Lord's gracious embrace in our grief, I expected a quick conception and return to what had been my version of normal. I never anticipated that the following cycle would yield another loss.

But the stretching wasn't over.

Loss accompanied loss with two miscarriages in two months and then followed the loss of what had always been. Conception had come so easily before; now it came to a full stop.

Month after month found me scrutinizing multiple dollar store tests, determined to detect the slightest evidence of hormonal hospitality. But no matter how strongly I willed it, my desperate desire couldn't manufacture that magical double line.

Month after month the questions stacked up like a fragile house of cards. Didn't God think I was a good enough mom? Didn't He realize that my time was running short? Would He never again allow us to nurture a newborn?

All the panic I had felt as a little girl trying to convince God of my fitness as a future mother surged fresh from my soul and swept me into hyper-persuasion mode. Wasn't I the one who had trusted God, and accepted a bounty of babies from His hand? Hadn't He put this desire in me from as long ago as I could remember? I vainly clutched these two proofs—one in each fist— as ammunition to convince God that I had no business not being pregnant. Surely God would agree that it was high time to halt this trial.

When my maneuvering and posturing failed to force God's hand, I came to the end of my pasted-together patience. One evening I paced in my room, dry-eyed but with fists balled in frustration until the indignation that had been slowly building erupted from my heart. "THIS IS UNACCEPTABLE!" My brain screamed what my mouth still didn't dare utter as my boiling emotion propelled me from one corner of the small space to the other. It was quite a declaration from a "don't-dare-give-God-a-reason-to-use-the-target-on-my-back" kind of girl.

I was genuinely shocked by the mutiny that rose up with hands on hips and a haughty glare. There it stood in all its rebellious glory, while I cringed under the audacity of it. It had been unleashed and I couldn't stuff it back into some safe little box. My goody-two-shoes self was forced to face a defiance I hadn't realized existed.

And it was a doozy of a defiance. God controls the womb. I had banked much on that and wasn't about to waffle on that reality. The solution was brilliant in its simplicity. Since God controls the womb, my mission was to control God. I wasn't okay with how He was running things. I wanted life to look like I imagined it—my way, my will, my agenda. No miscarriage, no loss or pain, and a growing baby nestled securely beneath my heart. And I wanted it yesterday. Was that too much to ask?

God could exchange my misery for merciful relief. He only had to say, "be still" to soothe this storm. As much as I wanted Him to, as much as I had tried to get Him to, He didn't utter those words to my circumstances. And I wasn't ready to hear Him whisper them to my heart.

I stopped my pacing and threw myself facedown—a quivering heap on the bed. I still didn't cry, equal parts frustrated at God's unreasonableness and frightened by my insubordination. Eventually, darkness swallowed the last light outside and pressed in through my window while I lay there, steeping in heartache and rebellion.

A NEW KIND OF LOSS

Secondary infertility swooped down and snatched away my cherished ideal for the timing and spacing of our children. It even nipped at the heels of my identity. Pregnancy is what I *did*. Mothering was my main gig. I was blindsided by loss and grief and railed against the inability to conceive. I wrestled. I rationalized. I fought. I cried. But despite my impressive tantrums, God refused to cooperate with my carefully-crafted agenda.

Infertility hurts. I carried a growing, squirming anguish instead of a growing, squirming infant. The ache swelled full-term at the end of each disappointing cycle. My heart bled raw every month along with my womb. Maybe it seems ridiculous. My life was full and blessed. I had nine beautiful children and a husband who was crazy about me. Without a doubt, the daily occupation of caring for and doing life with the family God had given me helped to buffer the blow. But still, I longed for more.

Many couples would gladly trade their brand of barrenness for the title of *secondary* infertility. They have no children and no guarantee that they ever will. I don't pretend to claim company with their suffering. But adversity isn't a competition. In God's economy, all suffering counts. Distress doesn't require a minimum number to register as valid on some suffering Richter scale. No matter the level, there is still real pain involved, and real grieving.

Months of hoping, mourning, and yielding once more to the Lord in devastating disappointment forged an understanding and empathy in me with those who don't receive what they so desperately desire. In one form or another, most of us have been there.

IMPATIENT SCHEMES

Abram and Sarai (later to be renamed Abraham and Sarah) knew what longing was like. Genesis chapter 16 relates their story. They had been married for many years but had no children. What they did eventually have was a promise from God: Abram's descendants would be as numerous as the stars (Genesis 15:5). When they received this news, the couple must have rejoiced and excitedly anticipated the pregnancy that they had always longed for.

But weeks turned into months, and months turned into years. They seemed to make no progress and come no closer to their anticipated desire. Finally, ten years or so after the initial promise they became impatient. At ages eighty-five and seventy-five, a baby seemed like a distant dream, so Sarai came up with a socially acceptable but ill-advised suggestion. Hagar, their Egyptian handmaiden, could bear them a child.

It wasn't uncommon at the time for a slave to become a surrogate, allowing the mistress of the house to assume the title and position of mother. This type of arrangement invited a full share of complications along with the added entanglement of conception occurring the old-fashioned way rather than in a petri dish in a lab.

Of course, things didn't go well. When Hagar became pregnant and proud, Sarai's jealousy burned. She blamed her husband and treated Hagar harshly. Abram and Sarai's efforts to accomplish God's promised outcome in their own timing and own way resulted in bitter conflict. Abram had a son by Hagar, but that son was not the promised child. In the end, they all suffered because of unbelief and a refusal to wait.

SEARCHING FOR A SOLUTION

We can all relate to the impulse that drove Abram and Sarai. When we find ourselves painfully stuck, usually our first response is to look about for a solution. We live in a DIY society, so often we attempt a quick fix. We tell ourselves we've got this. A little more effort combined with just the right steps, a firmer tug on those bootstraps, and we'll be on our way. It's the American way.

For those of us who long for a baby, this predicament-fixing mindset is big business. The fertility clinic beckoning down the street offers an opportunity to *do something* with a dizzying array of procedures to hopefully help us accomplish our goal.

There's good and bad news here. On one hand, we have

wonderful medical intervention that can help restore and heal the natural function of our bodies. But here is the caution: Sometimes we take things too far. And sometimes we jump ahead of God.

Sarai's solution was socially acceptable just like fertility medicine is socially acceptable in our culture. But for Sarai, the socially acceptable option wasn't the Lord's good plan. Sarai's actions indicated that her heart had become impatient and scheming rather than surrendered. As I grappled with secondary infertility, I could certainly relate.

Brad and I are not at all against doctors, medical intervention, or even searching for solutions. There is a legitimate place and time for seeking help, but the fertility center wasn't a recourse we felt free or called to pursue in that season. Instead, we needed to reaffirm that God was Lord of the womb. He, not medical intervention, was our hope.

Just as acknowledging His sovereignty over the womb initially required the step of faith to put aside our birth control, in the same way, our faith step at this point was NOT to act. Recognizing the striving in our hearts, we realized that for us, pursuing fertility treatment options at that time would have been God-usurping rather than God-honoring.

So, we determined to trust the Lord's plan...and wait.

WAITING WHEN WE CANNOT SEE

Sooner or later each of us will be required to wait. I don't know a single person who enjoys a forced delay. But in this life, waiting will always remain a reality. Some pauses lead to a predictable end; if I stand in the Walmart line long enough, I'll be able to purchase my cartload of groceries. If my son remains patient until his turn, he will enjoy riding the scooter. Waiting in expectation of a reasonably sure outcome isn't fun, but the attainment of the anticipated end softens the inconvenience.

The more challenging type of waiting holds out hope with no guarantee of our desired conclusion. We don't know what will happen or how long the wait will be. Standing still when life and time seem to be rushing by is an agonizing kind of difficult. Brad and I had to constantly remind ourselves that God is in control and that He is good, even when we had no tangible evidence that He would bring about the thing we desired.

Waiting often feels exasperating or even random, but rushing to a quick fix isn't the answer. We can be assured that Jesus never wastes our time, our grief, or our suffering. He uses it all for our benefit and His ultimate purpose (Romans 8:28–29). I had trusted Him enough to receive many children from His generous hand; now I needed to trust His generous heart toward me in this season of withholding.

I was surprised to realize I still had a lot of growing to do in this area. I thought I had surrendered my childbearing issues to the Lord, but I discovered I had only approached the matter from one angle. He had graciously enlarged my heart to value and desire what He calls valuable. It was right and good to embrace God's passion for life and I loved that He had led us to trust Him to give us many children. I was all in and standing on what I assumed was the right side of the issue. But issues are never the main point. God is. Our surrender isn't to a cause or an ideal. It's to the living God.

A WISE FRIEND AND A WHITE FLAG

Pat patiently listened to my complaining while she rummaged in the refrigerator, pulling out fruit and chicken salad for lunch. Her children were grown, and her house always felt calm and welcoming—no toys strewn on the floor or sticky messes adorning the countertops.

I made no attempt to help her but instead slumped at the table, occupied with my grief and uncertainty. "Do you think we will have any more babies?" I asked haltingly, my elbows on the smooth dark wood of the table, my chin resting on an open palm.

As Pat opened the oven door, the buttery aroma of warming croissants spread through the kitchen and mingled with the sweet autumn breeze coming in through the open window. She paused in her preparations and moved toward the table. "Yes, darling, I do." Pat laid a reassuring hand on my shoulder.

During the months of waiting, Pat had prayed with me, cried with me, and encouraged me to remember God's goodness. She had also compassionately spoken the truth. Pat sat down in the chair next to me, took my hand, and once again gently led me to the crux of the matter. "Remember," she said softly, "if it pleases You, Jesus, it pleases me."

I knew what she meant. Pat used that phrase often in reference to abandoning her desires in favor of God's much greater plan. If I was honest, my new normal, non-pregnant status didn't please me one bit. I wanted to hear her say, "yes, I think you'll have another baby," and ignore the reminder that "you can choose to be pleased with God's way even if it conflicts with yours."

Despite my struggle, I agreed with Pat's assessment as I sat at her table that day. I even dutifully attempted to embrace it out of good-girl compulsion, careful to align myself with what I knew was right. I didn't realize it at the time, but my wrestling heart only gave passing consent—just enough to convince myself that I had surrendered. My white flag flew primarily out of obligation rather than as an act of worship. I substituted a halfhearted resignation for the freedom of true release.

Don't get me wrong. I genuinely wanted to please the Lord. I wanted my heart and mind to line up with His good will and way. But I also desperately wanted another baby. These two desires warred within me—constantly creating confusion and tension. I knew the right things to say and do, but I couldn't manage to make them stick. My heart would circle back around to a desire stronger than I had ever fought against.

I waited because I had no choice. I wrestled with the frustration of my inability to gain what I wanted along with the guilt of knowing that my heart desired the gift more than the Giver. Like Abram and Sarai, I struggled and schemed, trying my best to figure out how to fix my pain while still perfunctorily acknowledging the Lord's sovereignty in the situation.

WAITING WELL

Waiting isn't a static, stagnant position. We can't plop down and indulge in a "wait strike" until we get our way. Waiting usually requires the mundane movement of faithfully doing what is next. I'm not referring to a frantic busyness that masks the pain or adds to the fallacy of our self-importance. I'm simply advocating a steady cooperation with the necessary movement of life. Often, waiting well looks like leaving the desire alone and steadfastly doing what needs to be done right where we are.

The laundry still needs washing, supper must be prepared, and the school assignment is due in the morning. No matter how urgent or important our desire is, normal life requires attention. As we wait, we tend to the responsibilities we already own. Faith moves to the sacred and often unremarkable rhythm of loving God and loving others in the midst of ordinary life.

Waiting also calls us to prayer. As I waited for another child, I begged the Lord to intervene. In the beginning, my petitions moaned and whined with frustration. But it was a start. I knew that God was attentive and tender toward me, and I trusted that He would use even my most feeble appeals to prod me along and finally move me toward the calmness of a yielded heart.

Sporadically, I embraced that calmness, and my groaning gave way to worship. The pain persisted, but I felt His peace spread like a refreshing blanket of praise over my weary soul. The Scriptures encouraged me to "continually offer up a sacrifice of praise to God, that is, the fruit of lips that give thanks to His name" (Hebrews 13:15). Praise is a sacrifice requiring faith and obedience when everything in us strains toward our desire. Worship acknowledges that God is good and that He knows what He is doing even when we are wounded and confused.

Those times provided respite, but the next week, the next day, or sometimes even the next moment witnessed my stubborn struggle rising again. I felt like my emotions were engaged in a never-ending whack-a-mole game. As soon as I slugged my insurrection with the hammer of surrender, another defiant desire popped up to take its place.

Over and over, I forced myself to reiterate the truth each time my will battled for supremacy. I rehearsed His goodness and released my good longing, struggling to calm and content my soul with His kindness. Desire never diminished, but eventually, my mutiny-filled moments dissolved more quickly. Grief puddled around my heart, yet a greater stillness and satisfaction in Jesus eventually permeated my spirit. I reminded myself repeatedly that He alone could satisfy, and that He promises to be found by those who diligently seek Him (1 Chronicles 28:9).

I knew Him, and yet, I stretched out to know Him more. *Lord, Psalm 63:3 says that Your lovingkindness is better than life—and that includes even precious new baby life. Please be to me all that You have promised—all that You are. Bless me, Lord, even me!*

As my heart cried out, reaching for the Lord and for a baby, I realized I was in good company. This particular pain has been a struggle for thousands of years. The Bible tells us of Sarai, Rachel, Hannah, and Elizabeth, women who loved God and waited on the blessing of a child.

Eventually, the wait ended for each of these women and the Lord graciously answered. For these particular ladies, His answer was "yes." In His perfect time, God acted on their behalf and did what only He could do. I love the tender words Scripture uses to describe the bestowing of the blessing. The Lord "took note of Sarah," and "did for [her] as He [had] promised" (Genesis 21:1). "Then God remembered Rachel"—not in the sense that He had forgotten her, but in the sense that He was acting on her behalf —"and God gave heed to her and opened her womb" (Genesis 30:22). The Lord also "remembered" Hannah (1 Samuel 1:19). He "looked with favor" upon Elizabeth "to take away her disgrace" (Luke 1:25).

God tenderly takes note of us too and sometimes He grants what we so fervently desire. Yet when God's answer is "no," His intentions toward us remain just as tender. Brad and I were still sitting in uncertainty—wondering if the wait would reveal God's lovingkindness toward us in a "yes" or a "no." But either way, we were slowly beginning to believe that just as God is always good, life without more children could be good too. We were learning to be content and enjoy the blessings He had given, rather than focusing so often on what we still wished we had. And the Lord was meeting us there.

RELEASE

Finally, my sorrow and struggle reached a crescendo one day while I was visiting my mother. I sat engulfed in my dad's big recliner, feeling like a bewildered little girl. Surrounded by the familiar family photos on my parents' wall, the damp nudge of their dog's questioning nuzzles, and my mom's gentle voice of reassurance, I confided the fears and pain I hadn't allowed myself to articulate.

The miscarriages felt like my fault. If only I could have done something, but I had no idea what. Had I failed in some way to protect those babies? Was it my fault that I wasn't conceiving? Was there some deficiency in me or some remedy I should be pursuing? What was I missing in this confusing equation?

As I poured out those thoughts to my mom, the burden of

culpability finally released its grip on my heart, as surely as my puffy eyes released the silent, steady tears that slid down my cheeks. I couldn't fix any of this. I knew that, but against all logic, I had still assumed the weight of responsibility and guilt—essentially claiming a level of control that wasn't humanly possible and that I hadn't even realized I was carrying. To everyone around me, it probably looked like I had relinquished all these things when we stopped using birth control. It looked that way to me too, until the Lord revealed the true state of my heart.

At last, I realized and admitted that I had never really resigned as manager of Laura Hinchman Childbearing Central. I couldn't control any of the mysterious wonders surrounding the intimacies of life. My posturing, begging, guilt, and brokenness were ploys and weights I hadn't handed to Jesus. It was time to let go.

That day I fully cast myself on Jesus. He had chosen the outcome of those two pregnancies, as well as the barrenness of the last months. If there was some course of action that I needed to take, He was big enough and He loved me enough to let me know. I could let go of the uncertainty and stop torturing myself with the what-ifs or maybe-I-should-haves. Weeping in my dad's big chair, I finally let go of my illusions.

That episode of realization and surrender didn't solve everything. My pain remained achingly present. The dance of longing and disappointment still swayed to the rhythm of my menstrual cycle. But I no longer attempted to manipulate the Lord or heap false blame on myself. I could finally accept His invitation to be still and know that He is God (Psalm 46:10).

This new stillness allowed me to walk in a measure of relief. I didn't trust my own heart, but the striving diminished and the sweetness of my joy in the Lord occupied much of the energy I had previously spent on speculation and struggle. I still cried often, but I recognized the nearness and comfort of Jesus.

THE ULTIMATE WAIT

Anna knew what it was to wait for a child. No, she didn't expect a pregnancy. In fact, she was an elderly widow (see Luke 2:36–38). But she waited in anticipation of THE child—God's promised Messiah.

Anna worshipped her Lord—praying and fasting night and day out of her love for Him. And God allowed her to recognize the infant Jesus when Mary and Joseph presented Him in the temple.

Of course, anticipating the coming of the Messiah was the most momentous wait of all time. Infinite God broke through time and space to grace this broken creation exactly as foretold by the ancient prophets. The promise of a Deliverer never wavered, but slowly and steadily it moved ever closer to fulfillment— woven in and out of Israel's inception and difficult history and finally fanning out to include all people. Over and over the Old Testament pointed to the One Who would one day enter the womb of a virgin and embrace the pain and humility of humanity to offer Himself as the way, the truth, and the life (John 14:6). The wait was long; the anticipation excruciating. But at just the right moment (Romans 5:6), Jesus arrived, died on our behalf, and rose again in victory (1 Corinthians 15:3–4).

Since then, we continue to wait for Jesus and His final return. Like Anna, we can wait expectantly until we enjoy the ultimate fulfillment of His kingdom and our final freedom from sin, sorrow, and death.

In the meantime, we all face unmet longings, like I longed for a baby. Whether or not we receive what we wait for, Jesus works on our behalf—skillfully shaping the circumstances and *us*. The more we learn to wait and surrender, the more we see that Jesus is the true aim of all our waiting. We begin to recognize His beauty and the beauty of all He gives. Faith tenaciously grabs hold of Jesus and waits for *Him*. No matter what happens in my world, no matter how much I long for a certain outcome, Jesus is the ultimate fulfillment of every promise (2 Corinthians 1:20) and every desire (Isaiah 26:8). He alone meets our deepest longings. He offers Himself, along with abundant life—whether or not that life looks like we anticipated. Jesus is our beautiful heritage.

And He is always worth the wait.

Taking No Offense

EMBRACING THE BEAUTY OF NOT KNOWING

*These things I have spoken to you, so that in Me you may have
peace. In the world you have tribulation, but take courage;
I have overcome the world.*
John 16:33

In December, a bit weary of the emotional merry-go-round
that twirled at the speed of my monthly cycle, I found myself
looking forward to a quiet Christmas with my family. For the first
time in a long time, I felt that I wouldn't be crushed to find out
that I wasn't expecting. Instead, I yearned for an emotional break
and the stability of simple contentment. It was time to focus on
advent, on family, and on the blessings so evident in my life.

I looked forward to our annual traditions—choosing and deco-
rating the tree, making sugar cookies, and reading our advent
devotional each evening. Brad and I savored these moments with
our children, and I was glad for the distraction from the ongoing
upheaval of infertility.

In the months leading up to this holiday season, I had been
checking to see if I was expecting even before my period was due.
In fact, that had been my pattern for years. By ten days or so after

ovulation, I would take a pregnancy test, sometimes seeing that sweet confirmation, sometimes needing another day or two for the proof to materialize. I had continued that pattern during the last several cycles, even as test after test revealed that I had not conceived.

This month, I didn't rush to take a test. I merely waited for my period to start...until it didn't. Could it really be that when I was least expectant, I was expecting? My heart held its breath and my hands shook as I placed the test on the vanity, but I hesitated to look lest it shatter my fragile hope. This moment could not be rushed. In the stillness that can only belong to a winter morning and a surrendered heart, I once more offered my hope to the Lord and rallied the nerve to look. Double pink dashes peeked out from the narrow window, shyly but surely announcing a sweet anticipation. A baby, a baby, a baby! I bounced on my toes and laughed out loud then rushed to tell Brad the news.

The rejoicing at our house that evening sounded and tasted sweeter for all the months of waiting and wondering. God had finally answered our countless prayers. A new little Hinchman was on the way.

The next several days I moved cautiously, sneaking around in hopes I could somehow evade disaster, praying that I wouldn't start spotting, and pleading with God for the life of this child. A week passed uneventfully, so I began to relax and prepare our household for the sickness that would soon move in.

It showed up just as expected. Christmas Eve dawned lively with anticipation, and a good dose of reassuring queasiness. We celebrated that God had blessed the world with His Son, and had blessed us with a child too. Our joy twinkled brighter than the lights on our tree.

Early January arrived, and along with it, my first OB appointment. I answered the questions, held out my arm for the blood pressure cuff, offered my vein to the greedy collection tubes on the other end of the needle, and stood on the scales in my sock feet. I knew the drill and was pleased to be back in the familiar world of slightly antiseptic smells and pregnancy charts. My nausea was constant but still relatively low-key at seven weeks gestation.

Our months of waiting and heartache were finally over. As Brad and I were escorted to an exam room, a giddy relief bounced back and forth between us. As we waited for the doctor, Brad speculated on how this little one would fit into our family dynamics.

"The boys are winning," he said, referring to our current count of five boys and four girls. "I wonder if this baby will even things up?"

I raised my eyebrows a bit skeptically. "Maybe, but that would mean three girls in a row. We've never done that before."

"Well then, the boys may solidify the lead at six to four." He grinned and reached for my hand. Neither of us had a preference. We were just glad to be back in a position to guess.

The doctor ambled in, offered his congratulations, and chatted through the usual pleasantries while he prepared to take a quick peek at our baby. The warm gel, the hand-held doppler, and the screen set up beside me were all comfortably familiar. We focused on the flat display with anticipation, always happy to see our child at any stage. But the image that appeared snatched us out of our euphoria and shoved us back into the grief and pain that had been home for so many months. There was no heartbeat merrily blinking up at us. The doctor said the baby looked perfect for five weeks, but I was sure of my dates. Our child was seven weeks old and should have displayed a beautifully beating heart.

To say we were blindsided would be an understatement. The queasiness that began right on time had reassured me that this baby was doing well and growing strong. Without the spotting I had experienced with my earlier miscarriages, it never crossed my mind that there would be any problem.

Neither one of us cried. I guess the shock was too fresh for that. But the pain took root in our hearts and sent stinging tendrils down through every recess and appendage. Grief once again saturated our weary souls.

We slumped into our car, silent on the drive home, already exhausted by the weight of this fresh sorrow and searching for words to frame the news to our children. Clutching the truth that God never makes mistakes and He is honored when we trust Him despite our pain, we gently explained the baby's death to the kids and encouraged them to trust God with their heartache also. Telling the children was always such a tender task for us. We knew they were hurting and didn't have the benefit of walking with God as long as we had. But we knew God would care for our children's vulnerable hearts and work in their lives as well as our own.

Our family of eleven divided up and piled on the couch and loveseat, a jumbled mass of intertwined laps and arms and tears. This was a shock to all of us. Three-year-old Lydia told us she didn't like it when babies died in my tummy. Abigail and Philip asked questions we answered as well as we could and finally, the focus became the ultimate of human questions: *Why?*

NOT TAKING OFFENSE

Since God usually does not grant an understanding of the why of our deepest griefs, I don't tend to waste a lot of time asking that question. From my perspective, this child and the other babies I miscarried should have lived. We should have enjoyed a lifetime of loving and teaching and praising God with them. But that's not what happened. No amount of intellectual reasoning, emotional wrangling, or soul-searching could satisfactorily explain to this mother's heart the *why* of my pain.

Jesus is able to heal and even to raise from the dead. He chose not to extend life and health to these dear ones of mine. He is able; He chose not. That is the crux of the matter. And that has been a struggle for as long as people have populated this post-Eden, pain-filled earth.

Even John the Baptist was not immune to these wrestlings. He devoted his life to pointing the way to the Messiah. He voluntarily decreased while Jesus increased (John 3:30). He spoke the truth in difficult and dangerous circumstances. But where did this faithfulness land him? In Herod's dungeon.

Lonely and bewildered, John sent a message to Jesus, asking, "Are you the Expected One, or shall we look for someone else?" (Matthew 11:3). In other words, if you are God's chosen one, why am I still in chains? Didn't I serve you well? Why wouldn't you rescue and deliver me? John grappled with the why of his situation to the point that he doubted who Jesus was.

And Jesus's response? Go tell John all the miracles I am performing—"the blind receive sight and the lame walk, the lepers are cleansed and the deaf hear" (Matthew 11:5). Jesus offered no explanation or encouragement. He simply pointed to the proof of His miraculous power and uttered this brief caution to the gathered crowd: "And blessed is he who does not take offense at Me" (Matthew 11:6).

Jesus knew it would be easy for us to question His motives. He can heal. He can save. He can deliver. But we all know someone who has held the hand of a cherished friend wracked by cancer, grieved over the destructive choices made by a loved one, or waited seemingly in vain for God to act on her behalf. Sometimes He seems unmoved by our pleas. We can choose offense—resentment when Jesus doesn't use His power to fix our problems in the way and timing we desire. Or we can trust His wisdom and His way and cast ourselves upon His compassion.

Honestly, if I could understand the why—if God laid it all out before me and showed me His purpose, His glory, and the eventual benefit of my hardship—that comprehension might not be enough to keep me from turning away from adversity if the choice was mine. I suspect that my weakness and desire to alleviate pain would trump the greater good. Even Jesus, in His humanity, asked the Father to let His cup of suffering pass (Matthew 26:39). He didn't want to endure humiliation, pain, and death on the cross. But greater than His desire to avoid those things was His desire to accomplish the Father's good plan. So, "for the joy set before Him [He] endured the cross, despising the shame" (Hebrews 12:2). It is only in His strength that I can walk through pain in a way that pleases Him.

So how did we communicate that to our children, looking to us for answers to the unanswerable? We simply told them that we didn't have an explanation, but that it was our privilege to trust God even when it hurts. We hugged and cried and grieved as a family. Brad and I couldn't take away the pain or fix their confusion, but we prayed that God would minister to each one of our children in their sadness. And then we tried to carry on as normally as possible while what I really wanted was to curl up and hide from the ache of our loss.

HOLDING ON

The next practical issue dealt with the fact that even though our baby had died, I was still carrying her. My previous dread of spotting became a desperation for evidence that I had begun to bleed. My temp was still up, indicating a healthy amount of progesterone, and it didn't seem to be in a hurry to drop. But I knew that if my body didn't expel the baby on its own, I would have to have a D&C (dilation and curettage) surgery. Forcing open my cervix and scraping my uterus didn't sound like a good plan to me and I cowered in fear at the prospect, feeling like a child who wanted to run and hide. Psalm 32:7 became my constant mantra: "You are my hiding place; You preserve me from trouble; You surround me with songs of deliverance. Selah."

I wanted my body to release this child gently and spontaneously, without the need for medical intervention. I couldn't stomach the thought of such a callous farewell to our precious baby. I was also concerned about protecting my womb for the possibility of a future pregnancy.

God, in a way I've never experienced before, please be my hiding place and my shield. Use all of this in a tremendous way in each of our lives. Please do not let one single stab of pain be wasted. Only You can heal us, God.

Two days later all I could manage in my prayer journal was a single sentence. *O God, I am your wounded child.*

It's a strange thing to be pregnant, but without life growing inside. I walked around knowing our baby had died, yet caught in some kind of strange gestational limbo. I was still queasy and frequently dry heaving. My womb held tightly to the child it had yearned to nourish and nurture—vainly offering sustenance and clinging to its mission with tenacity. It's not a scenario I desired, but I continued day after day in hopes of avoiding the medical procedure. I wanted to protect this fragile child whose soul no longer lingered here. So I waited, carrying her and asking God to carry me.

I returned to the doctor a week later to confirm our sad news. I still refused to consider a D&C at that point, so my physician gave me three more weeks as a deadline. Another week passed with no sign that my body would expel the child on its own. I became more agitated and desperate—begging God to allow me to avoid the surgery. Surely, He wouldn't ask that of me on top of everything else.

Paradoxically, normal life made grieving more difficult and also eased the process. While all this was going on, we continued to homeschool and maintain our typical routine. Isaac celebrated his thirteenth birthday and Lydia her fourth. We potty trained Hannah, and Brad was in the middle of a huge career decision, requiring lots of prayer and seeking the Lord. It was difficult to focus on any of these events in the midst of the pain, nausea, and uncertainty, but these everyday issues also helped us feel more grounded and kept us from being consumed by our grief.

REASSURANCE AND INEVITABILITY

On Monday, January 30, my heart still shrank back at the thought of surgery and all it represented to me. After our typical get-everyone-in-bed-and-settled drama, I snuck to the bedroom, silently crying out to the Lord for deliverance. I sat on the bed, my back touching the smooth walnut wood of our antique head-board, and wrapped myself in a blanket against the chill of the room. I rubbed my palm back and forth over the coverlet, switching the direction of the green nap several times before reaching for the Bible on my nightstand. The worn pages felt soft to my fingertips and the verses comfortingly familiar as I pored over previously underlined passages.

I came across Psalms 4:8: "In peace I will both lie down and sleep, for You alone, O Lord, make me to dwell in safety." I closed my eyes and spoke the words out loud, cautiously testing my reaction to their truth. I could lie down and sleep—even the induced sleep of surgery—in peace, knowing that He would keep me safe. I didn't want the ugliness of surgery to touch our baby. I didn't want the invasion of my womb. But sitting there on my bed, newly reassured by the promise of His presence, I knew God would probably require it. And I could sleep in peace because He would be with me.

The days plodded toward the inevitable. I experienced the Lord's comfort, but my distaste for the surgery and the over-whelming grief didn't abate. Finally, a night in early February marked the convergence of two highly emotional events—Brad resigned from his job to begin a new position with a much smaller company, and the D&C loomed large for the next morning.

I moved woodenly that evening. The air seemed to press

against me, too heavy to maintain its usual buoyancy. My responses were slow, my words sluggish, and even my thoughts required a moment of suspension before settling into a recognizable coherence. Initially, I attempted to salvage a sense of normalcy for my children, but I soon gave up the charade. And then I simply sat.

Before long, Kristy, a casual friend from church, arrived on our front porch, bearing a meal, a hug, and a sympathetic ear. She had heard from a mutual friend of my miscarriage and the required D&C. Having previously walked through the same situation, she could relate to my pain and dread. Her generous reaching out and ministering to me reminded me of God's tender regard toward me. Her warm voice, her embrace, and her empathetic understanding embodied the words, touch, and compassion of Jesus. I was reassured of His love through her love.

Still, the morning couldn't help but come. And neither could my mourning.

At the hospital, I began weeping. I could feel the tears assembling at the corners of my eyes, resisting, but ultimately succumbing to the swift slide down my cheek and then the three-inch freefall from chin to collarbone. Was God catching even these tears in His bottle, as David suggests in Psalm 56? I didn't bother to wipe them away. I couldn't muster energy for a gesture that seemed useless.

The staff wasn't quite sure what to think of me; I surprised myself, too, since I'm not typically a publicly demonstrative person. I had cried and grieved at home, of course, but something about facing the surgery and the finality of bidding goodbye to our baby signaled a rare permission for emotion to rule the moment. I sat on the edge of the stiff bed, gazing down at the pattern on my hospital gown with blurry eyes, clinging tightly to Brad's strong hand. My weeping was quiet but constant, not abating in the least as the nurses asked me questions. What time did I last eat? Was I in any pain? Did I understand the procedure and what to expect? I mostly nodded in response with an occasional mumble thrown in.

Finally, one nurse tentatively asked, "Why are you crying?"

I shook my head and choked out, "I just want my baby." I couldn't explain why this moment was so agonizing. Grief simply moved in and took over.

The teardrops kept up their steady vigil as the IV needle pierced my vein and the tape anchored it securely to my wrist. I lay on the bed, looking up at the tall pole and the steady drip, drip, drip of the attached line. Brad remained at my side, stroking my tear-wet hair and praying quietly until the clang of the side rail locking in place and the hitch of the wheels announced the time of my departure. Because of my obvious dismay, Brad was allowed to stay with me, against typical protocol, until they wheeled me toward the operating room. I turned my head for one last glimpse of his face as I rounded the corner with fast-walking, blue-clad sentinels on either side.

Later that afternoon, I rested in my own bed, attended by both fresh grief and reassuring relief. The procedure was over and had gone well. I was a little uncomfortable, but mostly I was overwhelmed with thankfulness that the Lord had seen me through this. I felt cleansed. I'm still not sure how to explain it; I knew my womb was clean, and somehow my heart felt clean too. My heart's surrender had grown full-term and given birth to a stillness and confidence in God's hand.

I didn't know what the future would hold. I still had more grieving and recovery to face. I still longed for a baby. I still also had my daily, lovely life with my dear ones, but most of all, I had Jesus. And I knew my surrender pleased him. At the moment, the joy of that realization was enough.

COMFORT

The surgery was the climax of an aching, painful period—a season of confusion and shattered hopes. But God was right there with me. To my surprise, the difficulties I dreaded didn't hold the power I'd imagined. They didn't destroy me or drive me further than His love could reach. His specific grace complemented my specific trial—like peanut butter complements jelly. And that grace granted a calmness and peace beyond explanation.

I'm not brave enough to choose pain. But I've seen that God can be trusted through my struggles and that He often reveals Himself in fresh ways through difficulty. In this instance, through the pain, I experienced God as my Deliverer. This time the Lord did not deliver one of my babies; nor did He deliver me from the situation. But He proved Himself my deliverer through the whole miserable ordeal. "For what I fear[ed] [came] upon me" (Job 3:25). God took me places I never wanted to go, but He gently held me through it. I felt loved and even cherished.

I used to hate taking my children for their immunizations. The nurse wanted me to hold them while she administered the shots. I didn't like that idea at first—a happy baby in my lap, smiling and cooing, suddenly surprised by the sharp, unexpected needle. I didn't want my children to think that I was the one who caused their pain.

Later I realized that I wouldn't have it any other way. As their mother, I wanted to be the one holding and comforting my children. I was the one they trusted. I was the one who could best console and soothe them.

Yet, as their mother, I was also the one ultimately responsible for what was happening. I didn't administer the shots, but I gave the permission. My children had no understanding of why I would allow such a thing. They had no concept of my desire to keep them from greater pain or danger. They had no clue there could be anything beneficial in that needle. I acted out of my love toward them, but they were incapable of grasping the reasons why.

In the same way, the Lord oversees all the unfathomable details of our lives. He allows the grief and sorrow that I cannot even begin to understand. But I can be still and allow myself to be comforted by Him. The reason for the pain is beyond me, but the means of comfort and healing is still within reach. I can sit in God's lap and be consoled through the sting, confident that He has my best interests at heart.

"WHY" WORKS BOTH WAYS

Difficulties are part of the brokenness of this fallen world. We are right to expect hardship—often without knowing the reason— and to entrust ourselves to God in our suffering (1 Peter 4:12,19). But *why* works in the other direction too. Why did God allow us to adopt? Why did He bless us with nine beautiful children before a first miscarriage? Why had He lavishly poured out on us grace upon grace? I can't answer those *whys* either, but I'm so thankful that He chose to bless us.

When there is pain and grief, we hunker down and cling to Him. He occasionally gives hard gifts which will prompt us to grow in perseverance, character, and hope in ways that ease could not accomplish (Romans 5:3–5). When He gives a joyful gift, we say thank you and do our best to enjoy those endowments. God is a gracious, giving Father who delights to delight His children. Either way, all His motivations toward us are tender and gracious. We may not understand the reasons behind either the difficult or the delightful, but we can trust His heart and intentions toward us.

It all comes back to faith. Most of the time, we won't recognize any evidence of good or benefit surrounding the origin of our pain. There are some mysteries in this life that we must leave in His capable hands. We choose to trust in His kindness, despite the glaring conflict between what our earthly eyes see and what our limited understanding can fathom. We walk by faith, not by sight.

God took me where I never wanted to go, but He tenderly held me and lavished on me the fortifying balm of His perfect grace. He supplied what I needed when I needed it. I still mourned the loss of my child. I still longed for a baby to keep, to raise. But I trusted God's work in my life. I trusted His goodness toward me. And I trusted that He was still weaving my heritage into something exquisitely beautiful.

A Double Portion

~~~

EMBRACING THE BEAUTY OF ABUNDANCE

The Lord has done great things
for us; we are glad.
Psalm 126:3

I woke early on my fortieth birthday, nervous about what the morning might bring. It was the eleventh day after ovulation in my cycle and I planned to take a test. Maybe, just maybe, God had a birthday surprise ready to be discovered.

With the stick lying on the side of the sink counter, I waited for an answer. I folded my arms and paced as much as our small bathroom allowed, refusing to speculate on whether excitement or disappointment would soon be my companion. I had slept fitfully, knowing that I would face this moment of truth. I suspected I was pregnant, hoped I was, but my intuition needed verification. Stealing a glance at the test didn't reassure me so I plopped down on the toilet seat lid, hands clasped and foot tapping impatiently while the secondhand moved slowly around my watch. A peek at two minutes gave me no reason to rejoice.

Disillusioned, but determined to see it through, I waited a final minute before picking up the bearer of bad news to verify that the test was negative. I knew it was silly to think God would give me a special gift on this day, but I had been hopeful in this first full cycle after the D&C.

I fell to my knees on the cold tile floor in a physical acknowledgment of what was going on in my heart. The disappointment was sharp, but I conceded once again that God is the One who always chooses well.

Father, I had so hoped for good news today. Nevertheless, not my will but Yours be done. You know best. Thank you for this moment when I can again confess that You are good and You do good. That is always good news.

I stood and brushed off my knees, resolved to enjoy this birthday despite the ever-present sadness. There was always next month.

It was still early in the day, so I quietly puttered around my room for a bit—making the bed, dressing, and finally pouring out my emotions in blue ink on the pages of my journal. I went back into the bathroom, the test drawing me like a moth to a flame. I always had to look again, just in case.

To my surprise, I discerned the slightest shade of coloring where the indicator line should be. Blinking my eyes several times and studying the stick from different angles didn't make the faint line disappear. I clutched the wand in my fist, afraid to fully embrace my building hope. Several minutes had come and gone and the line was a mere shadow compared to the nice solid mark I preferred to see, but my body was definitely producing hCG. I was officially pregnant!

I wish I could say that every ounce of me rejoiced. Brad and I were excited, of course, but we hesitated to allow our emotions free rein. Somehow it felt like we were protecting ourselves if we didn't expect too much or show too much enthusiasm.

Even though Brad and I were nervous about the outcome of this pregnancy, we broke the news to the kids and enjoyed their uninhibited delight. Heavy paper and colorful markers along with the mandatory Minnie Mouse shirt announced our newest blessing as we stood in a group outside my parents' house to let them in on the news. We swapped hugs and congratulations and posed for pictures, caught up in the excitement of what God had done—hopeful but still a little wary.

I carried a nervous energy along with our baby for two weeks until the not-so-subtle signs of pregnancy sickness hijacked my body. Nausea and frequent bathroom trips gave me some reassurance, but I wanted to see for myself that this child was thriving. At seven weeks, Brad and I braved the doctor's office for that fateful first peek inside my womb.

We were escorted to a room, already occupied by an ultrasound monitor sitting silent and foreboding, intimidating in its detached ability to impart gladness or grief. I looked around the small space, briefly noticing the colorful patterns on the wall and a bulletin board full of thank-you notes for babies successfully delivered. A dull nervousness in the pit of my stomach reminded me of the significance of this moment as I climbed onto the table. The doctor set about his preparations and coaxed the screen to life. I hesitated for a moment, searching out Brad's face before surrendering my attention to the monitor. There, inside an appropriately-sized sac, lay a bean-sized baby with a beautiful blinking heartbeat. I released the breath I hadn't realized I was holding.

Oh, thank you, God.

The doctor measured carefully, confirming our child's gestational age. "Looks like this baby is right on target with your calendar dates—officially due December 4."

My heart, previously beating as quickly as the baby's, now calmed into a reassured rhythm of joy. Brad squeezed my shoulder as we continued to stare at the screen.

"Everything looks perfect." The doctor spoke soothingly. "Let's check back again in two weeks just to confirm." Apparently advanced maternal age and three recent miscarriages made a convincing argument for caution.

"And...congratulations." He seemed relieved to say it.

We took our good news home with us and settled into the challenging parts of pregnancy. Despite how much I had prayed for and longed for this child, I still stumbled through my customary "I-can-never-do-this-again" moments. Everything was moving to the rhythm of my typical first-trimester groove. At nine weeks, we returned to the doctor's office for a second ultrasound. Once again, our baby showed off in all her healthy glory. My doctor declared that he was going to start treating me like a normal pregnant lady and would see me back in a month.

The weeks dragged by like they always did while nausea and vomiting made up my main pastimes, but finally, the calendar prompted us to once again make the drive downtown to the obstetrician's office.

SURPRISE! SURPRISE!

We anticipated a normal visit. I was thirteen weeks—just beginning my second trimester and satisfied with the reassurance of two previous ultrasounds along with the insistent sickness that refused to subside. To top it off, the baby twisted and turned in my belly as if on an amusement park rollercoaster. I had felt movement this early in several of my more recent pregnancies, but this child was a bona fide gymnast.

Since there seemed to be no cause for alarm, Brad and I entered the room with confidence. I relaxed on the table while the doctor squirted a blob of warm, clear gel on my already extended belly and began the slow sweeping motions that would cast the black and white image on the nearby screen.

Brad and I fixed our eyes on the monitor, expecting to see the silhouette and beating heart of our child. But instead, there was a surprise waiting for us. We had witnessed enough ultrasounds to interpret the obvious.

"There's two of them!" I gasped.

Brad and I looked at each other, eyes wide, hands clasped tightly, matching smiles splitting our faces. "TWINS!"

We once again turned our heads to soak up the two figures with wiggling limbs and beating hearts. The same screen that had so often indifferently revealed hard, sad news now heralded a lively joy. Two blessings, two beautiful babies, double the miracle.

"But how is that possible?" I could hear the incredulity in my voice. "We've had two ultrasounds showing only one baby." I tore my eyes away from the screen long enough for the doctor to validate this amazing wonder.

"I guess one was just hiding behind the other." He chuckled, caught up in our excitement.

Sneaky little siblings. That explained the almost constant party going on in my womb. I carried two little beauties swooping around, joyriding on that imaginary rollercoaster.

A PLACE OF ABUNDANCE

On the way home, we marveled at the privilege God had given us. How could *we* be the favored ones? How could our pain-filled waiting end in the glory that was this moment? Why did God choose *us* for this staggering honor?

Sometimes the wait ends in blessing that surpasses all expectation. Sometimes after the deepest mournings come the most magnificent delights. God is good when life hurts. God is good when the wait is long and the outcome unsure. And sometimes God's goodness spills over into beyond-all-that-we-could-ask-or-think abundance (Ephesians 3:20).

This unexpected blessing coursed through our hearts, carrying a sweet thankfulness and hope. Previously, I had grieved over the longer gap between babies, but now there were two to bridge the void. I mourned the babies we lost, but if the last one had lived, these two couldn't currently occupy my womb. The Lord had given, taken away, and now given again and He was not obligated to explain Himself. I couldn't begin to comprehend the why or how of this blessing. I had clung to the Lord in the loss and now I rejoiced in the gain—confident that both situations arose from the abundant lovingkindness of our God.

The kids watched from the front window and spilled out of the house as soon as we arrived home—eager to hover over the grainy ultrasound pictures they knew we would produce. We gathered in the living room giddy with the joy of our additional announcement. Once again, the roof rose an inch or two in the Hinchman household. The children's hootings and cheers and hugs and tears joined ours in raucous celebration. Then the race was on to see who could spread the word the fastest and farthest.

ABUNDANCE IN SCRIPTURE

Scripture's language is lavish. We have a generous God whose character and ways overflow with plenty. Over and over, we are reminded of the Lord's abundant lovingkindness (Psalm 86:5, Isaiah 63:7, and Lamentations 3:32 are three examples), His abundant strength and infinite understanding (Psalm 147:5), and His goodness (Psalm 145:7). God holds all power, knows all there is to know, and is everywhere at all times. Bounty emanates from the richness of His character and being. The Lord's very essence is abundance.

The Lord's blessings are also generous. God's gifts of abundance to us include redemption (Psalm 130:7), grace (Acts 4:33), pardon (Isaiah 55:7), peace and truth (Jeremiah 33:6), and supply for every good deed (2 Corinthians 9:8). We are even given the unsettling assurance of abundant suffering but also the comfort to match those griefs (2 Corinthians 1:5).

FROM GRATITUDE TO GRASPING

In addition to all these intangible benefits, the Lord's physical provision is often generous too. But Scripture tells us that there is an inherent danger that often accompanies physical plenty (Deuteronomy 8:7-14). Abundance can lead to amnesia. We forget who our Provider is and take for granted the blessings He has given.

Brad and I didn't have an abundance of possessions, but we enjoyed an abundance of children. We relished a sense of blessing and beauty with our large family that we wanted to continue and grow. We appreciated the gift of our children but had eventually moved from gratitude to grasping for more. It's a subtle trap—the enjoyment of God's abundance can easily turn into entitlement. We had spent months ensnared in that prison, and we had no desire to revert to our former misery. Our demands had finally subsided and our surrender and contentment had increased until we were satisfied with God and His provision for the size of our family. We were finally back to thankfulness for the wonderful children the Lord had already blessed us with regardless of whether or not He gave us more. Now, with our announcement of twins on the way, we didn't take for granted this miraculous blessing and privilege, or the One Who generously gave us these two sweet babies.

OPERATING OUT OF SCARCITY

But entitlement isn't the only temptation associated with abundance. Sometimes we go to the opposite extreme: operating out of scarcity. Both extremes set us up for failure and do not accurately reflect the heart of our generous God.

Operating out of scarcity leads us to buckle to the idea that there isn't enough, that the supply will run dry when we need it most, and that we will experience lack in damaging ways. The idea of scarcity causes us to fear and to make decisions that are not sound and wise.

In Genesis 3:1–6, Eve demonstrates the danger of acting out of scarcity. She was allowed to eat from any tree in Eden except the Tree of the Knowledge of Good and Evil. God's abundance was lavishly spread before her. The Lord met her every need and He Himself communed with her and Adam in the garden.

But the enemy convinced Eve of lack.

The serpent persuaded the woman that God was withholding good from her. So, at the serpent's prompting, she ate of the forbidden tree. As she swallowed, the sweetness on her tongue turned to bitterness in her soul. Her grasping sin stripped her of abundance instead of supplying her with the increase she sought.

Eve had freely benefitted from unimaginable plenty, but she believed the lie that the God Who loved her didn't have her best interests at heart. She took matters into her own hands, and we still tend to do the same.

In the spring of 2020, the coronavirus effectively shut down our country. Non-essential businesses were closed and people were asked to practice social distancing and shelter at home through the end of March. Then the order was extended for several more weeks in most areas. As soon as the measures were announced, the fear of scarcity compelled people to grasp and hoard. I walked through the aisles at Walmart, amazed and somewhat alarmed at the empty shelves where hand sanitizer, disinfectant cleaners, food items, and even toilet paper used to sit. Dread of not having enough drove individuals to snatch up more than they needed—more than was necessary.

Fear took over and took too much.

In our affluent society, we are used to grocery stores stocked to the hilt, beyond the imagination of any citizen in a third-world country. We turn on our faucets and reliable, clean water flows freely. We typically don't have to scratch and scramble wondering how we'll feed our children their next meal. But we can still struggle with the idea of scarcity.

Part of trusting God with the number of family members who would inhabit our household included trusting Him with the provision to meet the needs of those family members. We never had the suggested special college savings accounts, but through scholarships and provision at the right time, so far, our children who have wanted to attend college have been able to do so. They don't attend fancy universities, but they have done well and earned degrees from local schools while living at home. God has provided money for braces when needed. Our vehicles are old, but we have the transportation we require. We have always had enough.

During this pregnancy, we knew our bedroom space was getting tight. Where would we put two more? We didn't stress about it, but we needed to make some adjustments. I was encouraged by the truth of Psalm 84:3: "The bird also has found a house, and the swallow a nest for herself, where she may lay her young, even Your altars, O LORD of hosts, my King and my God." If the Lord provided a place for the birds to lay their young, He would provide a place for the children He gave us.

We finally moved two dressers out of the girls' 10 x12 room and into our slightly wider-than-usual hallway to make space for their cribs along with the two bunk beds already residing there. That gave six little girls a place to lay their sweet heads. None of us felt lack. We simply made room for the babies and didn't worry about space we didn't have.

I'm not suggesting that more space wouldn't have been nice. We house-hunted off and on for a few years, but didn't have the resources to purchase what we thought would be a good fit. Sometimes my soul longed for visual, physical, and emotional white space, but my larger desire was that there would always be room for one more. The Lord gave us creative ways to store what was needed, and we gladly chose the blessing of more beautiful family members over temporary comfort and convenience. Paradoxically, we didn't feel too crowded. God seemed to stretch our space each time He stretched our hearts.

We always had enough—enough love, enough space, enough grace to live together and love and forgive. Our enough was abundance. If we needed more, God would provide. We had what we needed at the time, and we had the assurance of future provision from the One who graciously provides all things.

TIME TRIALS

Even as the space issues worked out, something I struggled with as a mom of many was the idea that I didn't have enough hours in my day. Time always felt scarce. There never seemed to be enough of *it* or *me* to go around. Even though I had learned to relax to some extent and enjoy life without having everything done, I was and still am a Martha at heart (see Luke 10:38–42). I can quickly become distracted—"worried and bothered about so many things" (Luke 10:41). To sit at Jesus's feet like Mary requires an intentional act of faith. Given the incessant needs around me, a few moments of stillness and prayer often feels like an indulgence with the potential to send the projection of the day barreling straight toward chaos. But Matthew 6:33 assures me that if I "seek first His kingdom and His righteousness, [that] all these things will be added to [me]." Refusing to look around in panic, rejecting overwhelm at the start of each day, and intentionally slowing my mind, heart, and body to avoid a frenzied pace are all acts of worship and trust in the abundance God offers.

Jesus could have wrestled with time too, but he always moved unhurried, unhindered, and confident in what His Father wanted to accomplish through Him each moment. The press of a crowd, the confusion of His followers, and the constant needs of the world around Him never caused Him to lose focus on what was essential.

His example encourages me. Even with all my many distractions—the laundry piling up, the voices whining for dinner, the toys multiplying unhindered on the floor—I can accomplish exactly what the Lord has for me each day. I can feast on Him, I can love on my children, and I can serve those whom the Lord brings to my door, all with the assurance that I will have what is needed to minister in Jesus's name. And sometimes He even gives unexpected moments to clear the floor or catch up on laundry.

Abundant life no matter the circumstances is part of our beautiful heritage as believers. Brad and I experienced abundance during a season of loss and pain and uncertainty because the Lord favored us with a stronger, richer knowledge of Himself. We burrowed into a deeper place of intimacy with Jesus and experienced the quiet joy of His steadfast presence. And as will always happen when we see Jesus more clearly, our priorities and focus were realigned.

Now we were experiencing the abundance of generous blessing and fulfilled desire. This was a rich, bountiful time. We were expecting twins. All our other children still lived at home. I was still able to become pregnant and carry a child despite the previous months of heartache and waiting. These were the last glory days of a sacred season and I embraced this time for the sweet spot it was.

Forty was perfect. Forty was a time of abundance and anticipation. Forty was twins and rejoicing after a time of pain and waiting. Forty was the birth of Elizabeth and Esther on the one-year anniversary of the due date of the first baby we lost to miscarriage.

EVERYTHING WE NEED

"Hey, Laura." Susie's breathless voice carried down the hallway as she jogged up with a baby in her arms and a three-year-old zigzagging in front of her. Her two elementary-age children accompanied her, wiggling out their impatience as they shifted their weight from foot to foot.

Susie was a younger mom I was acquainted with from our church. She stopped me to ask a question about homeschooling curriculum. I'm no expert and I'm often at a loss to give specific advice, but I'm happy to share any wisdom God has granted in my years of parenting and homeschooling. I've gained a lot of experience in what not to do, and I've even scored a few wins. I've had some timely help from older moms too.

Susie and I chatted for a couple of minutes while she switched the baby to her other hip and we walked outside. Eventually, she sighed. "I wish I could be a fly on the wall at your house and just watch you guys."

I understand the impulse behind that desire. Sometimes it would be nice to actually *see* how fellow believers live out the ordinariness of their days. How are they faithful and how do they handle their mistakes? How do they practically love God and love others moment by moment? What does their parenting look like? How do they organize their daily tasks? When do they spend time with the Lord and, for goodness' sake, what do they have for dinner?

I invited Susie and her children over for an afternoon later in the week. We ate peanut butter and jelly sandwiches and browsed through my schoolbooks. Our children played together while we discussed schedules and chores and picky eaters. I also let her in on a little secret that we as moms often overlook when we see someone further along in their parenting journey while we feel like we are barely surviving.

I leaned toward Susie and reassured her, "If you were here all the time, you would see a lot of sin because a lot of sinners live here. But this is true, too: You would also see a whole lot of grace." Oh, the extravagant grace of God.

I am never going to be enough. No matter how much I want

to be the perfect mother. No matter how much I want to do everything right and love my family well. No matter how many times I pray that I will not miss something big and important going on in a child's heart or how often I desire to speak words of life and encouragement. I'm still going to be clueless about some things. I'm still going to speak less than graciously when I'm distracted or irritated. I'm going to sin, fail, blow it, mess up, operate out of my flesh—you pick the phrase. It's never pretty.

I know this is true, and yet I don't have to despair. I've received grace upon grace. I've seen God cover my mistakes. I've seen Him work in my children's lives despite my fumbling interference. I'm not offering excuses. I've often caused pain and hindered God's work in my life and in the lives of my family members. And those I love most have done the same.

Jesus offers "the forgiveness of our trespasses, according to the riches of His grace which He lavished on us" (Ephesians 1:7–8). What does that abundance mean? That we can live life to the fullest. That we can be free from sin and self and bitterness and hatred. That we can let go of the offenses committed against us. That we can rejoice and receive comfort even in suffering. That hope walks with us.

None of us will ever be enough. But Jesus always will be. The overflow of His abundant enough-ness allows us to repent and forgive and even spur each other on. I no longer expect to be perfect, and I'm learning not to hide in shame when I prove once again that my righteousness comes only from Him. I don't expect Brad to be perfect. I also don't expect that of our children. But praise God, Jesus lavishly shares His grace, beauty, and holiness with us.

When our scarcity of character or circumstance threatens to overwhelm us, Jesus is right there being everything we need. He is our wisdom (1 Corinthians 1:30), our righteousness (2 Corinthians 5:21), and our peace (Ephesians 2:14). He is our beautiful heritage. And that's an abundance we can bank on.

Waving the White Flag

EMBRACING THE BEAUTY OF SURRENDER

For it is God who is at work in you, both to will
and to work for His good pleasure.
Philippians 2:13

I sat on my bed with my heels propped on the narrow edge of the siderail, *World* magazine spread out on my lap. I was uncomfortably hunched over the magazine, too mesmerized to move, as I devoured an article called "Frozen Generation,"[1] highlighting the plight of frozen embryos. I had already been aware of the existence of these children in the earliest stage of development, and I had often pondered their predicament and wondered why the pro-life community was largely silent on the issue. When I found this article focused on the essence and extent of the situation, I couldn't stop reading.

As the author explained, "leftover" embryos from IVF (in vitro fertilization) procedures are frozen to allow couples a second or third try if pregnancy is not achieved on the first attempt. Couples who bear a child often thaw some of these embryos later, hoping to add to their family. Any of these tiny children whose parents no longer want or are no longer able to give birth to them face an uncertain future. Most of the time they remain frozen indefinitely—life in limbo.

It was late 2005, and the article claimed there were approximately 500,000 of these tiniest of humans locked in the freezers of fertility centers across America. Today, estimates place the number around one million.[2] But the Lord sees and loves these "forgotten" children, and as I cradled the magazine in my lap, He challenged me with the truth of what these embryos lacked: *All these babies need is a womb and a home—and you have both.*

He spoke so clearly that I was immediately suspended between the reality of my outwardly familiar surroundings and the equally real inner voice of God. My shoulders and head rose in high alert, my mind stood at attention, and my eyes closed in concentration. I noticed the faint vanilla scent of the unlit candle resting on my nightstand and the comfortable melody of family activity on the other side of my bedroom door. Every sense strained to full awareness in this divine commissioning moment.

I knew the Lord was speaking to me— that His majesty was breaking through to express Himself to my frailty. It was not in an audible voice, but in a penetrating, transformative thought. An unmistakable word from the Father to my mother's heart. My soul leapt in response, but I continued to sit, anchored solidly to the side of the bed in acquiescence and awe. *YES! Yes, Lord. We have what they need. May it be so.*

Adopting again had been a desire I'd held close to my heart for many years. It was a nebulous dream at best, with no real form or focus. And yet, I carried an unspecified awareness that it should be so. Might it be that the Lord would allow us the privilege of embracing some of these embryos as our own? Adopting at this earliest possible stage, I could give birth to and nurse my child. I loved the idea that even as an adoptive parent, I would be able to mother a child from the beginning.

At this point, I had a clear word from the Lord, but no specific direction. I wondered if I might be clinging to some self-fabricated hope. After all, this was 2005—right in the middle of our season of miscarriages and grief prior to the conception of our twins. I didn't trust my heart during this difficult time, and I feared that my desire for another child might easily supersede God's intention. Still, the Lord directly pointed out that *we* had what these embryos needed. I didn't want to erroneously assume that God would choose us, but my encounter with Him had been unmistakable. I held on to the sacred hope that He would somehow, someday give *us* that privilege.

With no obvious direction other than a trembling desire, I began to pray. Despite all I wasn't sure about, I knew that two things were true: God's heart embraced these little ones, and each one of these babies needed parents. Brad and I, along with countless other couples, had a womb and home to offer. I began praying that God would raise up many husbands and wives to parent these little ones, and that He would start with us.

EMBRACING SURRENDER

I couldn't wait to tell Brad about my encounter with the Lord. We snuggled into the overstuffed loveseat crammed into our small bedroom space—the one we hoped would allow snatches of private conversation in our nine-child household. The words spilled out, tumbling and churning like water in a swiftly moving, boulder-strewn stream. My hands moved in animation, my body turned sideways on the brown tweed cushion, as I poured out my excitement to Brad. But if my words mimicked a gushing torrent, his response quietened the stream into a cool, still pool.

Brad listened. He nodded in understanding, but no enthusiasm lit his eyes or lifted the corners of his mouth. "I need to hear this from the Lord," Brad said matter-of-factly, a settled expression on his face. I poked a bit, trying to discover any trickle of hope, but my husband was not captured by the idea of embryo adoption—not one bit.

My shoulders slumped and my hands grew still. Surely, he could see that the idea seamlessly integrated our love for children and respect for life. Wasn't it obvious? On the other hand, Brad and I had never considered ourselves risk-takers. We didn't jump into things on a whim; instead, we carefully considered our options and slowly decided our path, unless the Lord gave unmistakable guidance in a particular direction. Wanting a clear directive from God was not unreasonable for such a huge, life-altering decision. We needed to be in full agreement before moving forward.

Our impasse offered me an opportunity to surrender.

By this time, I had lots of practice in surrendering. God had used years of marriage, multiple children, and recent infertility and miscarriage, as well as the normal frustrations of life to school me in how little I could actually control. Fretting and pushing and nagging only kept me anxious and upset on the inside while accomplishing nothing positive on the outside. It's not that I had arrived in this area or that I didn't still struggle with it at times. But overall, the lessons God had so carefully built into my life, He faithfully helped me apply.

The Bible tells us to "Cease striving and know that [He is] God" (Psalm 46:10). This verse perfectly encapsulates *what* it means to surrender as well as the *why* of surrender. We can be still, stop wrestling, and quit manipulating when we comprehend, even feebly, God's existence and character.

Seeing the Lord put in place what was needed for our adoption of Ruth, trusting Him with our family size, and experiencing His comfort and peace as we waited and grieved over miscarriage and infertility all equipped me to lay this desire for embryo adoption at the Lord's feet quickly and without reservation. I couldn't manipulate the situation nor change Brad's heart. Brad's heart was God's job. Even when I didn't see movement or progress, I could remain expectant that what God had initiated, He would complete, without my input or interference. God was big enough to let Brad know in His perfect timing, and in the meantime, I could honor the Lord and my husband by not pushing.

Surrender is its own beauty. It declares that trust founded in the Lord is good and right. It presses into a realization that God's way and God's timing are far superior to our desires. Surrender isn't a grudging capitulation or defiant resignation that remains standing on the inside. Rather, surrender involves a true embracing of God's way. And yielding leads to the quiet joy of knowing that what we have chosen is pleasing to God.

God had spoken and I could rest, not knowing the outcome, but trusting that He was at work. I tucked that reassurance away for safekeeping, occasionally pulling it out to ponder and pray.

INFORMATION, PLEASE

Months became years, but my passion for these forgotten embryos had not waned. We remained busy, raising nine children, grieving through secondary infertility and miscarriage, and finally welcoming identical twin daughters. Just before the twins' first birthday, my cycles resumed and we conceived. Life felt like the good old days—normal and sweet. But the sweetness quickly turned bitter as we once again experienced the pain of realizing the precious child I was carrying had no heartbeat. Surgery to clear my womb was scheduled for Christmas Eve then Brad and I returned home to gather quietly with our family—simultaneously mourning our loss while commemorating the birth of Jesus.

Sixteen cycles came and went without a hint of God opening my womb again. I navigated the rise of hope and the fall of disappointment more smoothly than previously—without plunging into devastation. God had met me here before, during my previous months of infertility, and revealed His goodness even as He withheld the fulfillment of our deep longing. We desired and prayed for more children, but accepted not conceiving as our new normal. The idea of embryo adoption continued to flutter around the edges of my mind and heart, but for Brad, that butterfly remained snugly tucked into its cocoon.

More than three years after God spoke to me, the break-through came. In January 2009, I picked up a newspaper and read about an embryo adoption informational meeting sponsored by Bethany Christian Services, an adoption agency with a branch in our area. To my surprise, Brad agreed to go.

I called Bethany to reserve a spot. An acquaintance from our church answered the phone and I hesitated. Couples with eleven children don't call adoption agencies every day. But Peggy answered graciously and encouraged us to attend the gathering even though we would not be eligible to adopt through Bethany. Their program only accommodated childless couples for embryo adoption. The meeting would supply good information and then we could pursue other options with the NEDC (National Embryo Donation Center) located in Knoxville, Tennessee or our city's fertility clinic.

We entered the small room at Bethany's Chattanooga office. The cold evening in early February had required bundling so we shed our layers as we came inside, hanging our jackets on the stiff chair backs and glancing at the handful of other couples already present. Quick handshakes and introductions gave way to awkward pauses while we waited for the meeting to begin. Looking around, I read a cautious hope on each face.

The facilitator introduced herself and had each attendee do the same. At the gathering, there were two couples currently pregnant with adopted embryos. Hearing their stories encouraged us and one of the wives, Wendi, offered her phone number and her availability for questions. I left the meeting chattering about what we had learned and eager to find out more. Brad remained quiet and skeptical, but willing to hear what Wendi had to say.

A SERIOUS SNAG

I eagerly dialed Wendi's number, but by the time I put down the phone, my enthusiasm had evaporated. After the conversation, I understood enough of the typical embryo transfer protocol to realize that women usually take birth control pills for a cycle or two and that ovulation is routinely suppressed during the cycle of the transfer.

We hadn't prevented ovulation in nineteen years based on the parameters we felt God had established for us. Brad and I agreed that anything inconsistent with how the Lord had previously led felt like striving. Going on the pill seemed like a direct contradiction to what He had already built into our lives.

A quick call to the NEDC confirmed that they were unwilling to transfer embryos within my natural cycle. The practice is more common in other countries, but not the norm here in the States. Most doctors want to maintain careful control of a transfer cycle. The issue seemed insurmountable, so Brad and I both thought that God was giving us a clear refusal of the desire I had held for over three years.

Disappointed but yielded, I poured out my heart to the Lord in my journal: *After talking with Wendi yesterday I feel pretty sad. Unless You intervene or speak clearly, it seems You probably don't have this for us. Lord, my body and desires are Yours. You love those little ones and have good plans for each of them. If none of those plans include us, so be it. If one or more belongs in our home, then do what only You can do. This is a major hurdle.*

The next evening at church, I ran into Peggy in the hallway. We chatted for a moment above the usual hubbub from nearby classrooms, and I told her of my disappointment. "I don't think this is going to work out for us. The usual protocol requires suppressing ovulation and that feels like we are backpedaling from what God has already initiated in our lives."

Peggy paused for a moment. "Don't give up yet. Did you know

that Amanda, the embryologist for the local fertility clinic, goes to church here? You could call her and ask about any medical concerns you have."

My mind churned a bit with this advice and a spark of hope reignited in my heart. I was acquainted with Amanda but had forgotten that she worked at the fertility center. She would know if a natural cycle transfer was feasible. God might be providing a way. At least I felt encouraged that I had an avenue to keep gathering information.

"Thank you so much, Peggy. Maybe there's still hope." I gave her a quick hug and walked calmly down the hall while my insides bloomed with renewed enthusiasm. *Are You resurrecting this possibility, Lord?*

OVERCOMING HURDLES

A few days later I punched the keys and clasped the phone to my ear. I knew this conversation could be the final confirmation of a "no" answer or the beginning of God surmounting the insurmountable. I paced our hallway as the phone rang. The receptionist answered, and I waited to be transferred to the appropriate person.

Amanda received my interest in embryo adoption with enthusiasm, so I plunged into the nitty-gritty: "I've heard that common transfer proceedure requires taking birth control pills for a while to closely control cycles. Because of the Lord's leading in our lives, we haven't used birth control for many years."

I closed my eyes and stopped pacing before asking the crucial question. "Do you think one of the doctors would be willing to work within my natural cycle?"

Amanda paused for a moment before she replied. "I'll talk to Dr. D. I think he would be willing to work with you. Your next step would be to schedule a consultation with him and perform a saline ultrasound to make sure you don't have scarring or obstructions in your uterus that would inhibit the transfer and implantation of embryos. Would you like me to make you an appointment?"

I gripped the phone tightly, overwhelmed to hear that she thought it could work. "I'll need to talk to Brad before scheduling anything."

The warmth in Amanda's voice radiated through the receiver, fanning the flame into a sure hope. "Just let me know when you are ready," she said

I had been ready for over three years.

I wanted to follow the path further and see where it led. But Brad still loitered around the trailhead. His reservations were legitimate. Had God called us to this? If so, what were the ethical concerns? What medical interventions would be acceptable? These were questions we needed to answer, and we spent several weeks after my conversation with Amanda praying and hashing through these issues.

Even though I was anxious to move forward, I had concerns, too. The whole thing sounded like a sci-fi movie. One of the biggest apprehensions we had was with the full scope of what goes on at a typical fertility clinic. If we used their services, did it mean we agreed with or endorsed everything that happened under their roof?

Often, as a society, we take technology too far, without considering the long-term moral implications of our actions. Just because we *can* do something doesn't mean we *should*. And even among believers, there is much disagreement over what is acceptable when it comes to technology and fertility. At our local clinic, the embryologist was God-fearing and eager to protect the babies in her care. One of the doctors expressed the same life-honoring sentiment to us. But where their consciences demanded they draw a line was not necessarily the same place ours would land.

The gray area of reproductive technology begs for careful consideration. If God was truly calling us to the journey of embryo adoption, we had to know the boundaries that would keep our pursuit life-honoring and pleasing to the Lord. We needed to clearly understand our role, constantly surrendering the process and the outcome into His capable hands.

In the end, our adoption of Ruth helped us reconcile some of the struggles. We had not agreed with China's one-child policy or the government intrusion that encouraged countless baby girls to be aborted or abandoned. But our daughter was born there—an innocent victim of governmental mandates and difficult circumstances—and we didn't hesitate to bring her home. The steps we took to adopt her were in no way an endorsement of China's policies or government.

Similarly, there were embryos frozen in that clinic who needed a family. Transferring them into my uterus involved some specific steps that we found acceptable. That didn't mean we had to agree with everything that went on under the roof of the fertility clinic. In fact, we didn't even have to figure out what we thought was acceptable in the vast realm of reproductive technology. We only had to work out the parameters our faith allowed in this particular task.

NEXT STEPS

As we endeavored to flesh out a framework we were comfortable with, we soon realized we needed more information. We couldn't settle on specific boundaries until we understood more about the procedure and how it would physically affect the embryos and me. Brad was still reluctant, but he finally agreed that we could make an appointment—just to have some of our questions answered. The saline ultrasound would have to wait. This was only to chat with the doctor about the process.

I called the next day, eager to make an appointment, but I hung up the phone a little conflicted. I was excited to be on the schedule and making progress, but impatient at the s-l-o-w pace.

Amanda asked if we wanted to be put on the embryo recipient waiting list. As much as my heart cried *Yes!* I had to answer in the negative and simply be satisfied with this next step.

I realized enough about my cycle and the required ultrasound to know that the day of our scheduled appointment would probably be a good day for the test. It is usually performed between days 6 and 11 of a woman's cycle, before the lining in the uterus builds up so much that the contours of the womb can no longer be clearly seen.

Even though I was anxious to have the test and move forward, I kept my mouth shut and prayed. As much as I wanted to see where this adventure took us, I didn't want to push ahead of God's timing or feel like I was dragging Brad along.

Our consultation with Dr. D was scheduled for Tuesday, March 18. The morning witnessed our usual family activities and antics, but I finally broke free in time for a quick shower before our early afternoon appointment. Outside, the days were finally stretching beyond the confines of winter's grip, but the chill in the bathroom still called for some extra warmth. I reached past the blue-striped curtain to turn on the water—nice and hot.

All the while, I was thinking about how God had orchestrated Ruth's adoption. Brad and I were both certain from the beginning that we should pursue it. God had graciously given specific direction and confirmation to us both throughout the process. This time things were different. I stepped under the warm spray and let gravity weave the water through my hair and onto my shoulders as I considered the way the Lord was weaving this adoption together.

God had spoken to me about embryos that significant day in 2005, as surely as I stood in the shower. But then years passed as I continued to pray, without any visible sign of progress or reassurance that this was the right path. God remained silent.

Now, Brad's willingness to at least consider it, along with the removal of some early hurdles, encouraged me that the Lord was still at work. There was no direct, unmistakable confirmation that we were headed in the right direction, but as I pondered these things, I knew that we were. I carried an inward settledness in my heart. God had initiated this. All would happen in His timing. I only needed to walk forward as He orchestrated the details.

I turned off the water and reached for my towel with a steadily building excitement. I didn't know how long it would take, but I felt the reassurance of inevitability.

Brad arrived home from work to accompany me to the appointment. Ready to walk out the door, he hesitated for a moment and caught my hand to stop me.

With a slight shrug of his shoulders, he said, "So, I've been thinking. *If* the timing is right with your cycle and *if* the doctor has room in his schedule this afternoon, then I'm ok with having the ultrasound." Brad tried to appear casual as he spoke, but I knew the significance of his comment. God was continuing to work quietly behind the scenes in his heart.

"That sounds perfect." My words showed restraint in an attempt to match his off-handedness, but I squeezed a little more tightly than normal when I hugged him.

ON THE LIST

By the time we left the office that day, many of our questions had been answered and the ultrasound confirmed that there were no physical red flags to prevent embryo transfer. Brad hesitated a bit but agreed that it was time to take the next step.

We paused at Amanda's desk to give her the good news. "We're ready. Please put us in line," I gushed.

Amanda grinned and gave us a wink. "Between the time of your phone call and your visit today, two other couples asked to be put on the waitlist. So, I took the liberty of slipping you in first."

I could've done a happy dance right there in the fertility center hallway. I clasped my hands in excitement, willing my feet to be still and behave.

She consulted the papers in front of her. "You are officially seventh in line. Two groups of embryos are poised to be adopted. Three or four other couples are ready to donate." Amanda stood and came around the side of her desk. "It takes a month or two to complete the paperwork, but you should be hearing from us before long."

Amanda's words beat a joyful rhythm in my heart as we walked out of the clinic.

WAITING FOR INFORMATION

We were on the list. Brad had agreed to that, but with reservation. He sensed we should be moving in that direction, but there was one final hurdle that wouldn't let him rest. Brad was convinced that God would give us another baby conceived naturally, before He orchestrated an embryo adoption. I was more than skeptical since we hadn't been pregnant in a year and a half. We continued to pray and ask God to solidify all this, then we both settled down to wait—me with ill-concealed impatience in contrast to Brad's rising trepidation.

As normal life kept its pace, we often drove by the fertility center which faces a main thoroughfare near our home, though the building itself is perched a short way up a quieter side street. Each time we drove by the low, brick structure, we wondered about the frozen embryos housed there.

Many evenings and weekends we hopped on bikes, peddling through our quiet neighborhood, then winding along the narrow road that linked our street to the sidewalk lining the busy thoroughfare. Legs pumping and hearts racing, we would finally arrive at the clinic, gliding in circles around the empty parking lot while we prayed for our babies nestled in a freezer somewhere inside. They occupied a physical location and we were drawn to that location repeatedly, wanting to be as close to them as possible.

As we waited, we continued to pray and process, firming up what this adoption might look like. Embryos are frozen in tubes called straws. One of the women at the informational meeting told me that they had adopted seven embryos—four were on one straw, three on another. All embryos on the same straw must be thawed at the same time and if there are too many for a single transfer, the remaining ones are typically refrozen.

We didn't know how most embryos were grouped when frozen, but we felt strongly that our job was to unthaw these little ones and not refreeze them. That was one of the parameters we knew must be in place for us to proceed. It seemed that refreezing would expose them to unnecessary danger.

Most doctors are comfortable with transferring two embryos at a time—perhaps three at the extreme. Our desire was to transfer two. We didn't know how our embryos would be arranged, but if three were on a single straw and thawed, we would not refreeze the third. That was non-negotiable. The doctor would have to be willing to transfer all three in that situation. During our consultation, Dr. D had agreed to that, but we all preferred to avoid transferring more than two if possible. We loved the idea of twins again. But triplets? That made me gulp a little.

Having finalized most of the decisions surrounding the ethical considerations of embryo adoption, submitted to the required bloodwork, and explained our intentions to family, we had nothing left to do but wait. Weeks became months, and I itched to check in and catch a glimpse of how far the line still stretched in front of us. We had been told it wouldn't take long. Of course, "not long" is entirely relative, depending on whether you are on the arranging end or the anticipation end. Brad didn't want me to call the clinic for an update. He remained steadfast in his insistence that there would be another baby first.

Finally, at the beginning of August, my surrender stretched thin. I cornered Brad, pressing him to let me find out some information. I pushed shamelessly and steadily until I got my way. Brad remained reluctant but finally agreed that I could call—soon.

I never made that call.

AN UNEXPECTED TWIST

The urgency of "soon" faded as I stood in the bathroom, wide-eyed, watching a double pink line darken on a test stick. On August 14, Brad earned the right to say "I told you so," and I've never been so happy to admit that he was right. Nor so confused over what God was doing and what this could possibly mean for waiting embryos.

All questions aside, we were overjoyed to be expecting. We had prayed unceasingly for another baby even though I had assumed that would come about through adoption. We also tiptoed a bit through our excitement since four of our last five pregnancies had ended in miscarriage. I quickly made a first appointment with my OB, anxious to discover how this little one was doing.

Ten days later, Brad and I rode around for a while before the appointment, running an errand for his job and trying to quell our nervousness. Finally, Brad pulled the car into a gas station parking lot and twisted toward me in his seat.

"I need to tell you something." The tone of his voice communicated urgency. Brad leaned forward and his eyes locked with mine before he continued. "No matter what happens today—whether our baby is alive and doing well or not—I want you to know that this is the child I've been waiting for. This is the baby I thought God would give us." Brad sat back with the air of someone who had just made a big announcement, then raised his eyebrows expectantly.

I shifted in my seat, absorbing his words, aware of the

summer sun pressing through the windshield, trying to figure out why he was telling me what seemed obvious. Of course, this was the baby he had been convinced would come.

Brad picked up on my confusion and tried a different tactic. "I'm telling you that now that God has given us this baby, I'm one hundred percent on board with the adoption—whenever He orchestrates it."

I grinned big, finally understanding, but wanted him to say it again. "Really?"

"Really. Completely. One hundred percent." His declaration sang to my soul and then lifted as praise to the One Who was faithful to lead us forward. God had removed the last hurdle from Brad's heart. This baby was truly the reason he had dragged his feet. He hadn't wanted to miss out on this sweet gift, and now he felt free to fully embrace the next one, too. We were finally unified on the issue.

Clasping hands we prayed briefly together for the child I carried and the embryos that we would someday claim as our own. Then Brad turned the key, and we drove toward our OB appointment.

ULTRASOUND UNCERTAINTY

The ultrasound proved extra temperamental that day.

Megan greeted us cheerfully. "Are you ready to take a look at your baby?" She dimmed the lights, situated the wand, and gave her attention to the image in front of her.

She moved back and forth between what looked to me like two empty sacs and then focused for a long time on one of them.

I couldn't piece together what I was looking at. "Do you see the baby?" My hope was fading.

The technician bit her lip in concentration and didn't respond.

Silence is always a sobering guest in an ultrasound room and we could see no evidence of a pulsing heartbeat, so Brad and I both assumed our child had died. That had become an all-too-common reality for us.

In my grief, I prayed for Brad and the children and then began quietly praising God. *Father, once again You have given and taken away. Thank you for this precious, eternal blessing. Please comfort all of us in our fresh grief.*

My surrender and praise in this new sorrow was a sweet and pleasing posture before the Lord. It wasn't a superficial nod of agreement with what was going on in my life. It was a true sacrifice of turning to the Lord and trusting His goodness when everything in me cried out for a different resolution. His peace infused my freshly broken heart and seeped out to surround me with comfort and tranquility. Worshipping quietly in His presence, I felt securely held by the Lord.

Gradually, I became aware of the screen and the tech's presence again. What should have been a quick look to verify a heartbeat and take a couple of fetal measurements had turned into a twenty-minute marathon. Megan had still not given us an indication of what was going on, but she finally went back to the first sac, which looked empty until she enlarged the area. Immediately we saw the beautiful blinking of a tiny heartbeat! Relief merged with my worship and I released the tension in my shoulders. The Lord had not taken away what He had given after all. That was enough. We simply rested in the joy of the moment.

Megan removed the wand and wiped the gel off my belly. She offered a weak smile at our excitement then left the room abruptly.

The cause of her reserve became clear as the doctor entered the room. "Megan is concerned that you have a tubal pregnancy in addition to the one in your womb." Dr. C sat on the stool in front of us, but she didn't seem concerned.

My eyebrows rose in surprise. I'm not sure what I had expected to hear, but that wasn't it.

"That would be extremely rare, and I don't think you have

anything to worry about," she added, clicking her pen decisively, "but just to be on the safe side, I want you to go in for a more advanced ultrasound screening in a few days."

She jotted a quick note on my chart, then softened her voice, "Congratulations, you two. I'll see you back here in a couple of weeks."

Despite the unexpected report, Brad and I were elated with a healthy heartbeat and rushed home to share our happy news with the children.

That evening we went out to celebrate the life of this cherished child as well as a future embryo adoption. A double-baby bash! Two babies to look forward to and two hearts finally surrendered and unified in awe of what God was doing. We could joyfully declare with the psalmist: "The lines have fallen to [us] in pleasant places; indeed, [our] heritage is beautiful to [us]" (Psalm 16:6).

---

1. Lynde Langdon, "Frozen Generation," *World*, October 29, 2005, 26–29
2. National Embryo Donation Center, https://embryodonation.org/, 2022

Taking the Risk

EMBRACING THE BEAUTY OF OBEDIENCE

For this is the love of God, that we keep His commandments;
and His commandments are not burdensome.
1John 5:3

Thursday, September 3, 2009, dawned with reason to rejoice. Our twenty-first anniversary would start with a morning peek at the baby to confirm what I was confident of—there was no ectopic pregnancy. We planned to contact the fertility center that afternoon with news of our pregnancy and thus our desire to postpone the adoption until we could remove the "No Vacancy" sign on my womb. But as we had learned before, plans may change based on a darkened room, a glob of clear gel, and a fuzzy ultrasound screen.

The ultrasound was to be a more advanced screening performed in a location away from my physician's office. Brad and I entered the quiet, darkened room and marveled over the tiny, blinking heartbeat. After a few moments of enthralled oblivion, we noticed that the technician didn't offer congratulations or even a smile.

Her reserve disquieted me. "Is there a problem?" I asked

cautiously, not sure I wanted her answer to intrude on our excitement.

"The sac measures too small."

She didn't offer more, so I kept prodding. "What does that mean?"

"I really can't speculate. I'll send the results to your doctor. If you have any questions, ask her." Her words were clipped, her manner dismissive, indicating we would get no further information from her.

We drove home conflicted, unsure of what the news meant and what to expect. An internet search suggested that the outcome of our pregnancy could go either way. A small sac might mean nothing, or it might mean our baby wouldn't make it. Subdued by the possibility of another miscarriage, we decided to wait until after our next appointment before contacting the fertility clinic to tell them of my pregnancy. But in the irony that is sometimes God's timing, that afternoon, Amanda called us.

After months of waiting, she offered us our choice of two sets of embryo siblings. We explained that we were expecting, but that our ultrasound had been less than encouraging. We were unsure of our availability to adopt for now. Amanda graciously agreed to retain our place in line and send us the profiles and information on the embryos while we waited to see what would happen.

We went to bed that night desperately praying: for our sweet one nestled in my womb, and for the precious nameless babies frozen in the clinic, listed on paper, waiting for a family. *What now, God?*

The next day, Amanda faxed us the information on both embryo groups. We held in our hands two documents describing genetic parents, medical backgrounds, and history since conception. And we were supposed to choose.

The whole process felt strange and confusing. When we

adopted Ruth, China assigned each couple a child, so it was easy to trust that God would make sure we brought home the daughter He had chosen for us. At about the same time, I watched a friend agonize over the pictures and profiles of children as she and her husband navigated their adoption. Now we were the ones required to choose. And with much less information.

One of the sets of embryos listed two siblings—exactly what we had envisioned. Both babies would be transferred and securely implant in my welcoming uterus: twins. Everybody would win in our ideal, fairy-tale scenario.

But as I prayed, I was drawn to the group of five. *Five? How would that work? I can't carry five babies at once. Someone would still be frozen. Or worse, someone would die.* That sure didn't fit with our picture-perfect plan. But it was inescapable. As much as I wanted to claim the two, I had no sense of connection with them other than my previously constructed notion. However, I was inexplicably attracted to the group of five. They somehow just fit. They seemed to be calling me Mama.

Sometimes God speaks so clearly—removing doubt, waffling, and painful second-guessing. That's only happened to me a handful of times. More often He gently leads through His Word, through our desires, circumstances, counsel, or more of an unexplainable sense of direction. Our surrender and His peace allow us to move forward with confidence.

As I tried to discern where He was leading now, I wondered what Brad would think. We had decided to pray separately over the weekend and then see if we agreed on which set of embryos we were supposed to pursue. I couldn't logically explain it but felt confident that we should choose the group of five. Would Brad agree? Would God lead him the same way He seemed to be leading me?

We slipped away for a short walk to compare notes, but neither of us seemed in a hurry to speak first. We strolled silently for a while, absorbing the normal neighborhood sounds of lawn-mowers, birdsong, and children playing.

Finally, Brad spoke first, "Which set of embryos do you think are ours?" he asked, kicking a stray rock down the street while a small dog yipped at us from its front yard.

I swallowed hard. "I know it doesn't make sense with what we expected," I replied, searching my husband's face, "but I think we should choose the five."

"Really?" Brad left the rock and looked my way. His eyes were bright and the corner of his mouth lifted in a smile. "Me too."

Suddenly, we couldn't talk fast enough.

"I feel pretty strongly that they are ours. It's not at all what I thought." I placed a hand over my still-flat belly. "And I don't know what we are supposed to do if this baby is fine." My steps sped up as if propelled forward by my words.

Brad quickened his pace, too. "I don't know either. It seems like our role is to unfreeze the embryos as soon as possible. Obviously, we can't do that while we are already pregnant."

"Right. But I can't imagine letting them go." I stopped and turned toward Brad. He looked as bewildered as I felt.

"So, we will just keep moving forward and see what God does with all of this," Brad said decisively. "For now, I'm thankful He led us the same way." We continued our walk, grateful for unity and eager to see how the Lord would sort all this out.

Once again, God had proven Himself faithful. We agreed that the five embryos belonged to our family. The choosing was more subtle than someone putting a baby in our arms, but still unquestionably God's doing. We trusted that He would continue to orchestrate the next steps.

As all this excitement swelled, the precious child I carried constantly filled our prayers. Along with beseeching the Lord, I kept reassuring myself that our baby was thriving. *Surely our sweet pea is still doing well. We just saw her heart beating three days ago.* It was as if my inner dialog verified her well-being. *It's only been a few minutes since I last considered how well she must be, so of course, she is still fine.* This mental routine felt perfectly logical and comforting to a desperately hopeful mama.

Tuesday arrived, and we easily released the paperwork for the sibling group of two embryos. They were not our babies. But with each day that passed, we were more convinced, more attached, and more protective of the five. This was confusing to us because we felt that it was our job and privilege to unfreeze these little ones as quickly as possible, not keep them in limbo. But they would have to remain frozen for the duration of my pregnancy and a while afterward. We weren't sure how God would work all this out but felt confident that these five embryos belonged in our family.

On Thursday, I presented myself to the OB again. Strangely, she had no indication from the ultrasound report of the previous week that there might be something amiss. She treated our visit as a normal checkup and reassured us that everything seemed fine. Even my progesterone levels looked beautiful. At the last minute, she agreed to a quick ultrasound to put our minds at ease.

Grief showed up on the screen that day. I saw it in black and white before it settled solidly in the bottom of my belly. Realizing our baby's heart was no longer beating was a shock after our physician's cheerful optimism, and yet hauntingly familiar too. Brad and I clasped hands and held on tight. We knew what was coming.

Realities had to be dealt with and decisions made. I didn't want to wait this time. No prolonged delay of the inevitable. Surgery was not the best option, since we didn't want to do anything that might cause scarring in my uterus. This time I would take a pill. Dr. C offered her condolences along with a prescription.

I shuffled up to the window at the drugstore and handed over the prescription with a shaking hand. I managed to croak out my name and birth date before collapsing into one of the stiff seats along the wall. I wept—shoulders heaving, water dripping from my eyes and nose, sobbing audibly on that ridiculous blue plastic chair. Other customers shifted in their seats or busied themselves with their purses, discretely averting their eyes from my socially awkward misery. Finally, the pharmacist called my name. I clenched the sack she handed me and stumbled from the store.

Saturday was the day I physically bade goodbye to my baby. That's the day my body cramped and writhed in tandem with my heart—both working through the wrenching required to let go. All of me surrendered, exhausted with grieving and goodbyes and brokenness. Then finally, the stillness of acceptance after I released what I could not hold.

A WEIGHTY OBEDIENCE

Amanda called on Tuesday. Despite the heartache of our loss, I had embraced a determination that it was time to move forward. I wanted to make plans for the five we claimed as our own, and to make room for life and hope in the wake of death and grief. Amanda thought November would work well if my cycle normalized, and we were able to hitch a ride on the right timing. Papers would be signed later but it was confirmed: the embryos were ours.

Life returned to some form of normalcy as we began preparing our children for what we hoped would be another pregnancy soon —explaining the embryo adoption as clearly as possible to each age. We continued to process our grief as a family—mourning our loss and making room to risk again.

Before long, though, Brad and I also unwittingly welcomed the whispers of that formidable foe: fear. It began with the realization that this story might not end as we had imagined. There were no guarantees. Our obedience did not obligate God to deliver our "two embryos = two babies to raise" scenario. I knew that, and we had already foiled our ideal plan with the acceptance of five embryos instead of the two we had envisioned.

The often-grim realities of embryo adoption intruded upon our hearts. Usually, some of the embryos die in the freezing and thawing process. Implantation is no guarantee, and even if an embryo burrows into the lining of the uterus, miscarriage is still a substantial possibility. So many things can go wrong, and the pain of our recent loss cemented the difficult possibilities in an all-too-real way.

We were simply scared.

Brad and I didn't have doubts about the adoption. We knew God had led us and given us these babies. But we trembled at what might be required. Fear felt heavy, and apprehension haunted us.

We faced opposition on another front as well. My formally supportive mother did an about-face when she realized that we were planning to quickly move forward with the embryo trans-fers. I'm sure it's hard to watch your daughter suffer through multiple miscarriages. And the last one was fresh. She wrote us a letter expressing her concerns and asking a lot of questions, including the whopper of why we thought God was leading us to adopt in this way when He kept taking the babies He had already given.

I had no answer for that.

It did seem counterintuitive. I knew God had called us to rescue these embryos even though He had not allowed several of our naturally conceived pregnancies to come to term. His thoughts and ways are so much higher than ours (Isaiah 55:9). Some things we simply don't understand. But we can trust His goodness toward us.

I knew all this, but I was tired of the hurt, tired of the loss, tired of the painful possibilities. I was confident we should and would move forward, but I had trouble seeing much beyond the murky fog of fear. Brad was struggling with his own uncertainties, wanting to understand more of the physical process of embryo transfer and accessing the potential (and indeed likelihood) of loss. Instead of anticipation and joy, we both walked somberly during those weeks, pressed down by the weightiness of this obedience.

When I discussed these difficulties with my friend Pat, she gently reminded me that I was not offering the Lord that which cost me nothing (2 Samuel 24:24). Indeed, this obedience was an offering, and the cost struck at some of my deepest fears and longings. I could easily acknowledge that God was worth it, and the babies were worth it. I reminded myself of these truths often, but still fear was the stale air I breathed. And discouragement seeped out with every exhale.

The psalmist tells us that when he sought the Lord, "He answered me, and delivered me from all my fears" (Psalm 34:4). I longed for that deliverance too. I cried out and asked the Lord for reassurance and encouragement. I asked fervently and often. I longed for release from the grip of fear, yearning for fresh hope in this endeavor. And God answered in a big way.

FRESH REASSURANCE

The kids were temporarily occupied with their schoolwork and block building, so I slipped away to the bedroom. I pulled out my spiral-bound prayer journal from 2005, looking for encouragement from the Lord. I wanted to remind myself as concretely as possible how God had spoken when He first called us on this journey.

I flipped through the handwritten pages, searching for my record of the event, looking at dates to navigate my way. For some reason, I thought my encounter with the Lord had occurred in January, but as I flipped through my journal, I was surprised to realize it was much later in the year—October.

I found the entries from that time—vivid reminders of the

days that led up to that impactful moment. Earlier in the month, Pat and I had driven home together one evening after an extended day of fun, work, and rich conversation. In the quietness of the car, gliding through the settling dusk, I had attempted to explain the predicament of frozen embryos and my chagrin that the pro-life community wasn't actively advocating for them. Pat had never heard of the technology or the circumstances of these littlest ones. As I described the situation, one hand on the wheel, the other gesturing wildly, I had finally blurted, "What are we going to do about all those frozen babies?" I didn't have an answer then, but I couldn't keep myself from asking the question.

My eyes swept over the pages of my journal, the words igniting the passion I felt that evening in the car and then later as the Lord spoke. Sitting in the middle of the bed, with my note-book and the embryo profile papers spread out before me, I noticed the October entry date at the top of my journal page, and something clicked. Why did that date seem so familiar? I reached for the profile papers and quickly scanned the information. Hmmm. October 2005. My heart could barely register what my eyes had discovered.

Our five beautiful embryos were conceived and frozen the same month the Lord first spoke to me about them!

Even as God had begun to prepare my heart, He had given conception to my children.

Unknown to me, as I drove in the car with Pat that October evening, wrestling over the fate of babies frozen in limbo, God was watching over several precious, newly-conceived lives as they divided and grew in a petri dish at the fertility center two miles from my house. A few days later those embryos were checked for viability, put on straws, and frozen for a long winter's nap. On October 25, I read the article entitled "Frozen Generation" in World magazine and heard the Father Who sees and cares point out that I had what these babies needed—a womb and a home.

I should have realized it sooner. The dates were clearly indicated, but God had given me a gift and allowed me to unwrap it at just the perfect time. Our babies had been conceived and frozen the very month and year that God had first spoken to me about them, setting my heart on the path that had brought me here to this moment. I pressed the papers to my chest and closed my eyes in praise and acknowledgment of God's graciousness.

And all the fear fell away.

I had been given the privilege of praying for these babies from the beginning just as I had for our other children. My Father had allowed me to mother them before I knew they existed and were mine, and now—four years after their conception—I was finally ready to claim the embryos as my own. Worship and joy immediately swallowed up the heaviness I had carried the past several weeks, and the sweet realization of God's perfect timing and orchestration infused me with renewed resolve and excitement.

God graciously encouraged my husband also. The next day Brad called to tell me to listen to the Focus on the Family radio broadcast. The topic for the day was embryo adoption. When I called Brad back about halfway through the program, he was crying. God had reassured him also and reminded him that this calling was a privilege.

In less than twenty-four hours, the Lord had obliterated the fear and reluctance from both our hearts. We felt reaffirmed, loved, and strengthened, although nothing had actually changed but our perspective. The psalmist tells us that "all the paths of the Lord are lovingkindness and truth" (Psalm 25:10). There was still no guarantee that things would go as we hoped with the embryos; and yet, we had the assurance of God's lovingkindness —no matter the outcome. A path lined with that encouragement couldn't help but look pleasant. This was still a risky obedience, but we took the next step with determination and, finally, anticipation.

On Monday, November 30, 2009, two fragile embryos were transferred into my uterus. They entered at just the right time, as if they had traveled down my fallopian tubes instead of being introduced through my cervix. They were not aware of the ultra-sounds to check the thickness of my uterine lining, the blood-work, the progesterone shots, and the rest of the preparation needed to ensure their welcome. Or the prayer.

Earlier that morning the embryologist had painstakingly thawed the first straw. One of the two precious souls nestled there had died in the freezing process—our first loss. A third embryo on its own straw had been thawed so that two living embryos could be transferred into my womb, while the final two embryos remained frozen.

After all the prayer and preparation, the surrender and suffer-ing, the transfer procedure only took a few minutes. Soon I was back home, resting for the next several hours as required, satis-fied with our obedience and hopeful that both babies would successfully implant into the lining of my uterus.

None of us can measure the full significance of surrender, but that ordinary day in November produced some extraordinary results. Two embryos sought refuge in my womb; one fragile soul enjoyed the presence of her Creator; and one family prayed and waited to see the outcome of their obedience.

A few days later, the pregnancy test registered negative. We weren't particularly surprised. There was sadness, of course, but also a settled certainty that we had offered our best. We consoled ourselves with the fact that we had removed those babies from their frozen limbo and offered them a warm, hospitable place to thrive. I had mothered them well during the short time they were in my care. God chose the outcome, and even in our grief, we were content. We had done what we could do.

The medical community would not validate my experience as a miscarriage since the embryos never implanted. Without the crucial burrowing and attachment of implantation, there is tech-nically no pregnancy. But my mother's heart knew there were two tiny babies inside of me, and there was loss. So, I count them. Every precious life is worth counting.

December found us hopeful again as we monitored my next cycle. An ultrasound revealed that my uterine lining looked ideal, so the office tech drew my blood and set a tentative transfer date for the following Monday—just after Christmas. We left the center optimistic, brimming with expectation that soon our last two embryos would be warm and safe where they belonged. But God orchestrated a delay. The bloodwork indicated that my body would be optimal during the Christmas weekend when no one would be working at the clinic. Monday would be too late.

The embryo transfer would have to wait. Our raw emotions and disappointment were not-so-subtle reminders that following the Lord requires constant readjustment toward surrender and obedience. A simple truth, but rarely easy when hope is delayed. We offered the Lord our frustrations and determined to enjoy Christmas with our children.

Once more, in January, we approached the midpoint of my cycle with anticipation. Ultrasound, bloodwork, and progesterone shots again played the opening act in the intricate production. Sunday, January 17, 2010, was the transfer date—"gotcha" day in adoption terms. It was also Sanctity of Human Life Sunday. On that day each year, believers acknowledge the sacredness of every life and on that same day fifteen years prior, God had spoken to us about Ruth's adoption. The transfer date was a sweet realization of how the Lord had brought this issue full circle in our lives.

That morning, we arrived at the clinic anxious to hear if both of our babies had survived the freezing and thawing process. We were reassured that two babies would be transferred into my womb that day, and we were led back to the holding area in preparation for the procedure.

Amanda, the embryologist, entered the room and smiled at us reassuringly. "I have some bad news and some good news. First the bad: One of the two remaining embryos didn't survive the freeze and thaw."

I struggled to reconcile the report that two embryos would be transferred with what Amanda was saying. *Another one didn't make it; we've lost four of the five.* I licked my lips and shot a glance at Brad, before focusing my attention once more on Amanda.

"As we were retrieving your embryos, we realized that there were three more in that sibling group. The good news is that those three belong to you." Her tone was warm and compassionate as she looked from me to Brad and back again. "We knew you wanted to transfer two, so we went ahead and thawed a third embryo when the second one wasn't viable."

I waffled briefly between grief and joy, anguish and awe; another precious one lost and three more gained. "You mean we will transfer these two and still have two more frozen, waiting for us?" I could hear the incredulity in my voice. Brad just sat there grinning.

"Absolutely," Amanda reiterated. "They are yours." She closed the file folder in her hands. "Now, let's transfer these babies!"

After the procedure, I lay pondering and praying. *How could there have been eight instead of five? I don't understand any of it. But, oh God, thank you for entrusting them to us. Thank you for blessing us with three more precious lives. I am humbled and honored. I offer myself anew as Your beloved daughter and willing servant.*

He gave them to *us*. God could have chosen anyone, but He chose us. The wonder of that soaked in. At the same time, I faced the very real possibility that I would not be able to carry the two embryos just transferred to term. Somehow, I knew. We would have gladly given birth to twins and then come back for the last two as soon as possible, but I didn't think that was the role God had given us. Rejoicing tinged with sadness accompanied us home, but we prayed and clung to hope. God had proven Himself full of surprises and, perhaps, He would surprise us again.

At my next checkup, there was just enough hCG hormone to

produce a positive test. Implantation had occurred, but two days later the numbers dropped. Again, we braved the trauma of hope giving way to grief and consoled ourselves with the knowledge that we had offered our best.

Despite the sorrow and emotional exhaustion, I remained eager to jump back in and free our last two precious babies from their ice chamber. I longed to offer them safety and opportunity for growth. I also longed to give my heart the stability of a resolution to this adventure—one way or the other.

AN INTERRUPTION

While Brad and I had devoted three months to carefully tracking my cycles and praying, hoping, and grieving over these tiny babies, the rest of life moved forward with its own priorities. And life was about to press in with a twist.

In early February, my calendar rudely reminded me that I had a doctor's appointment to keep. For about five years, Dr. S. had been keeping track of my enlarged thyroid. Sometimes an ultrasound test would reveal that there had been no growth. Other times my thyroid would be slightly larger. It functioned fine, so I resisted having it removed (which is what my physician had said would eventually be required). At this appointment, he declared that I had waited long enough. He even gave me a twenty percent chance of having cancer.

So off to surgery, I went.

It wasn't that easy, of course. We agonized over whether we should transfer the embryos first. If I carried one or both to term, would I have to stop nursing to have surgery shortly after delivery? What if cancer resided in my neck? After much prayer and counsel, we decided that surgery first would be the wisest course. Even though Brad and I remained anxious to claim our last two embryos, we settled in for a lengthy wait.

We waited for the biopsy report that assured us I was cancer free. We waited for full recovery, and for time and bloodwork to determine the medication levels my body needed. We waited for my hormones and cycles to resume some kind of predictable dance. And all the while our last two embryos waited too.

Finally, in July, my body was ready. But we had one more delay as Dr. D decided I would need to have another saline ultrasound to check my uterus for scarring or any other impediment that would make it inhospitable to our delicate, needy hopefuls. Over and over, my desire to carry these babies had to be submitted to the One Who does all things well and to His perfect timing.

FINAL TRANSFER

Finally, transfer day arrived—Friday, August 13, 2010. Our remaining two embryos, both blastocysts (five-day-old embryos) had survived the thawing process. My mom, her reservations resolved, was in the holding room with us before and after the procedure. The click of the camera documented her excitement as well as the holy moments of our hopeful obedience. Would God allow us to parent these final two babies longer than the others?

Wednesday, August 18, found me squinting at a home pregnancy test, desperate to see that miraculous double line. It was early, but possible—5dp5dt (5-day-post 5-day transfer) is the same as 10 days after ovulation in a normal cycle. I'd had positive tests that early before, but I'd also been pregnant and not had enough hCG to trigger the hoped-for result. That morning, the test didn't cooperate. It's always discouraging to see a glaring empty space where you desperately desire a positive confirmation.

I squelched the disappointment enough to face the day and shuffled to the kitchen in my house shoes and robe to start breakfast. Another twenty-four hours would probably give a definitive answer. But the questions churned. *Am I pregnant or not? Why can't this be easier? What if all this doesn't result in a child to raise? Why in the world did I take a test today instead of waiting?*

I cracked eggs over the hot skillet vacillating between grumpiness and resignation. As I reached for another one, I noticed something written on the inside of the light gray cardboard egg carton. It was a Bible verse. *Really?* "This is the day which the Lord has made; let us rejoice and be glad in it" (Psalm 118:24). Today—this day of not getting the news I had hoped for; this day of not yet knowing the result of almost five years of prayer; this day the Lord gave for more waiting, more trusting, more surrender, more moving forward in steadfast obedience. This day offered an opportunity to simply rejoice. My assignment was to once again embrace the "not knowing" and rest in God's knowing, God's timing, and God's results.

I rejoiced that day when it wasn't easy. I rejoiced the next when the grin on my face could not be contained. Three positive tests, all different brands, hid gleefully in my bathroom drawer. The first heralded the good news, a second confirmed it, and the third I used just for the sheer joy of watching that line materialize. Again.

I poured cereal and milk for the children's breakfast and snuck back to peek. Still three lovely positives. After morning lessons, I checked again. I held each one in the light, gazing at the faint but unmistakable line of proof. Stunningly beautiful. They were the tangible evidence of God's secret work hidden deep inside me.

SORROW

Our euphoria lasted until the weekend. I took a test each morning and noticed on Saturday that the line was not getting darker, but a little fainter instead. My hCG seemed to be decreasing rather than increasing. It looked as if we would be facing a difficult grief.

Could this journey really be over? All the praying, the process, the pain, the surrendered risk, and desperate hope? Would we not have a sweet baby to raise? What now, God? I clung to the truth of God's word as if it were a lifeline: "How great is Your goodness, which You have stored up for those who fear You, which You have wrought for those who take refuge in You, before the sons of men!" (Psalm 31:19).

On Monday, I sat weeping in the waiting room of the clinic. The tech's compassion surrounded me as she drew my blood, but I refused to be comforted, convinced that our babies had died. The sensitive clinic test produced a beautiful dark line, but I was not reassured. The phone call that afternoon with the result of my hCG level was not bad news—86.3. The numbers were consistent with early pregnancy, but I knew what my simple home tests were showing. My hCG appeared to be decreasing instead of increasing.

On Tuesday night, I pulled a piece of paper from my Bible on which I had written some notes at random times during the past couple of years. Seeing the scribbled information took me back through the process. I read what I had written while on the phone with Wendi as she explained that she was required to take the pill for a few cycles. I had thought the Lord was shutting the whole thing down at that point, but He had made a way for us to use my natural cycle.

In another corner of the paper, I read notes written almost a year ago during my miscarriage when the doctor had given me instructions for taking Cytotec to clear my womb. My handwriting was shaky and hesitant. I teared up as the words made the details fresh—the uncertainty, the loss, the waiting, and the surrendering. In every phase, God had overcome obstacles and had given grace and peace. None of it had been easy, but all of it had been infused with His love and faithfulness. Now here we were at yet another crossroad on this crazy journey, wondering what was next and feeling raw and wounded.

On Wednesday, we took our feeble hope back to the clinic for more bloodwork, then we busied ourselves with the ordinary while we waited for the phone call. And we also waited upon the Lord. It's a curious thing to wait upon the Lord. To fervently pray for our cherished desires, knowing God can and may deliver, but also knowing He may not. And realizing that despite the anguish, it will be okay if He doesn't.

Our true inheritance is the Lord Himself and the abundant life He offers. A beautiful heritage is not dependent upon the fulfillment of my earthly desires—no matter how cherished they are—but on my relationship and eternal standing with God. I am loved by Love Himself and ultimately that is the truest reality and the greatest legacy possible.

I was in a much different place than the younger me who had mourned her first couple of miscarriages and then waited months and months with no conception. What once felt unacceptable was settled now. It's not that I finally understood. So many times God had revived this desire and orchestrated this process, and it didn't make sense to me that it might not end in pregnancy and birth and hopefully a lifetime of two children following and loving Him. But ultimately God would choose. I would wait on Him—for His answer and for the grace to accept that answer and whatever repercussions came with it.

The kids and I tackled our schoolwork for a while, then prepared lunch while I tried not to look at the white rectangular-framed clock on our wall. Finally, the phone rang and I lifted it to my ear with a shaky hand.

It was Dr. D on the line, and he wasted no time on preliminaries: "119."

I collapsed onto our old but comfy couch, deflated and dreading to hear the rest of his news.

Dr. D continued, "I wanted the number to be at least 142 [a 66% increase], but I really preferred closer to 172—double your number on Monday." He spoke a little more gently. "Come again on Friday and we will see."

I heard his attempt to soften the news, but it was obvious he didn't expect a better outcome when we returned. My hope plummeted. I knew it was over. These kinds of numbers usually indicated death had already occurred or was imminent. I no longer held any expectation that we would be able to raise either of these little ones.

We had traveled this risky road, and now we were facing a dead end. My heartache was too acute, too raw for any attempt to make sense of what was happening. I gathered up the pain, the confusion, and the heaviness as well as I could and crawled into God's lap to be held. Only He could fix this. Only He could fix *me*.

In addition to this fresh sorrow, I had to face the wider grief of realizing my childbearing years were likely over. God could still bless us with another child, but from a human perspective, at age forty-four, I knew it was unlikely. That realization called forth a deep sadness—one that I still feel keenly at times—but without the former struggle. Now that our almost five-year saga was ending without the birth of a baby, I was heartbroken, but I wasn't looking frantically around trying to manufacture a plan B. I was finally resting instead of resisting.

Our older children understood the implications and importance of the phone call, but the younger ones were still excited, rubbing my tummy and talking about how much fun it would be to play with the babies once they were born. I simply smiled weakly and pulled them in for a hug. There would be time to tell them later. Brad and I needed some space to grieve quietly and seek God about what might be next, and even how to explain to our children the unexplainable. I prayed that none of this would be wasted—none of the pain and confusion, none of what God intended to accomplish in our lives. That somehow through all this we and our children would love and trust Him more.

RETURN TO THE CLINIC

I stood staring at my reflection in the glass door of the clinic for a moment before walking in. So many times I had entered, hopeful and expectant about what God would do. Would this be the last time? How many hands had touched the same smooth metal of the handle, pulled open the door, pushed down desperation, and reached for hope? My eyes swept the tastefully decorated office—plants strategically placed around the room, books lining a shelf invitingly. The cheerful receptionist sat behind her broad counter with stacks of brochures over to one side. A couple already occupied seats in the far corner.

After a few moments, the technician called my name and led the way into the cramped lab occupied by a single chair. Brad stood just outside the door while I once again held out my arm for bloodwork, going through the same motions that I and countless other women had willingly endured for the hope of a baby. My heavy heart barely noticed the prick of the needle.

A few minutes later, I walked out of the clinic feeling old and empty. I didn't even attempt to stem the tears. Brad and I simply stood in the parking lot—not speaking, not praying, arms around each other in sad, subdued acceptance.

REJOICE AND BE GLAD

At noon we got the call. My hCG level read 222—an 86% increase! Dr. D was pleased and said maybe we just had a "slow grower." Brad grabbed my hands and danced around the room, exuberantly dragging my reluctant feet along with him. I was stunned and remained guarded and fearful, not trusting that it was safe to hope again. As soon as I could grab a quiet moment, I sought the Lord, yearning for His perspective. His word admonished me to "rejoice and be glad, for the Lord has done great things" (Joel 2:21). So once again I risked my heart. I chose to rejoice.

On September 7, we gazed nervously at the screen. One beautiful heartbeat blinked at us as we blinked back the tears. We breathed a silent goodbye to our seventh embryo and grinned a relieved welcome to our eighth. Hello, Baby. Due May 1, 2011.

Ezra entered the world in the usual way—with pain, pushing, and finally praises. He came to us as a whisper from God—an invitation of blessing and surrender—and his arrival in my arms felt like nothing short of a miracle.

The Lord had enabled this loss-fearing mama to willingly risk the pain that I so desperately wanted to avoid. Love dared to risk. Embracing the possibility led to the blessing. Willingness to "lose" gained us a son.

In addition to the gift of our precious boy to raise, we also gained seven other children—the embryos that the Lord created and called into His presence—to rejoice with in heaven. Our faith was fortified, our surrender strengthened, and our joy intensified. And all of this was grace.

This obedience had been risky for Brad and me because we didn't know what would happen, and it mattered to us—a lot. Would we give our all—our money, our bodies, our hearts, our hope—only to face a bitter outcome? We didn't know.

There is no guarantee in this life of faith except the guarantee that Jesus is certain and He is worth any and every obedience. We offer our best, we offer ourselves, and we wait for Him to do what only He can do—both in the situation and in us.

In one sense, obedience always feels hazardous. We follow without knowing exactly where we are going or how things will turn out. But in another sense, obedience is never truly a risk. It is always the right course, the sure path, the upward motion toward God and toward embracing our beautiful heritage. Obedience is our outward expression of love. And obedience is always worth it because Jesus is always worthy.

Epilogue: Generational Heritage

We will not conceal them from their children, but tell to the generation to come the praises of the Lord, and His strength and His wondrous works that He has done.
Psalm 78:4

Outside my window, the leaves are changing—announcing a change of season. They are still holding on, inviting wonder and excitement with a dance of new hues. Even though it's a little sad to let go of the long, lush days of summer, this new beauty beckons me with expectation and hope. Yes, things are changing. Yet this season holds promise and loveliness as surely as the last. It just looks different.

It took me a while to adjust when my cycles first began shifting and lengthening. I rushed to the dollar store for a pregnancy test each time I was late, until I finally realized that a late period no longer indicated the presence of a baby. It simply meant God was changing my times and seasons (Daniel 2:21). My body was winding down after a long fruitful summer. It wasn't my plan or preference. However, because of the previous months of waiting and our losses before the twins were conceived, I had already settled my soul in being satisfied with God's plan in this area. I was glad to leave behind the former struggles.

At the same time my childbearing years were waning, Philip married his sweetheart, Leah. Before long we received the joyous news that they were expecting our first grandchild. Our excitement grew as her belly expanded, and then, wonder of wonders, at age 47, I also became pregnant. This old mama had the joy of once again seeing those thrilling double lines. We had been blessed again! Sadly, an early loss determined that we weren't able to enjoy this sweet soul on our side of heaven. Meanwhile, our grandson flourished and was born at the proper time. Ezra, our youngest son, was two and a half when our grandson Bradley arrived. No, Ezra wouldn't have a younger sibling to play with but he would now have a nephew as his constant companion.

Since then, four more of our children have married, adding a total of four beautiful daughters-in-law and a son-in-law to our growing family. Eight lively grandsons and one sweet granddaughter fill our home with energy and antics. Two more grandbabies are due soon. And we will celebrate two more weddings in June.

For me, menopause has placed a permanent pause on my childbearing ability. I will never again carry a baby in my rounded belly or nurse a newborn. I've completed this leg of my race and passed the baton into the capable hands of my daughters and daughters-in-law. They are beginning their race. They grasp the stick and groan with the burden of bearing and raising the next generation. It's difficult, holy, beautiful work and the Lord will equip them step by step as He did for Brad and me.

Even though I can no longer bear children, my mothering duties are far from over. Ezra is now eleven. One moment he is reaching for independence; the next he reaches for my hand. Elizabeth and Esther, who just celebrated their sixteenth birthdays, are becoming confident young women. Hannah attends the local community college while maintaining a job and a grueling gym protocol. Lydia works full-time as a dental assistant and loves it so much that she is continuing her schooling in hopes of becoming a dentist.

Our adult children still need support and guidance too. Education decisions, parenting struggles, and career moves are just a few of the challenges they face. They are not immune to the highs and lows common to all who inhabit this globe. As they have entered into their own childbearing years, I've been privileged to see ultrasounds, witness births, and grieve miscarriages. It is an honor to walk with our sons and daughters through the mundane days, the difficult days, and the days of beauty and wonder.

My current season of life carries profound meaning and purpose. I have the assurance that I can still be fruitful in old age (Psalm 92:14), and that I can proclaim "to the generation to come the praises of the Lord, and His strength and His wondrous works" (Psalm 78:4). Continuing to invest in my children and seeking to influence my grandchildren is the high, meaningful calling of my older age. God designed the most important things —eternal things like faith and love—to be passed on through family. Heart to heart, moment by moment, slowly and steadily as we share life together, we are imparting truth and legacy. We are speaking about and living out abundant life in Jesus. Our words, our example, our life invites the next generation to "taste and see that the Lord is good" (Psalm 34:8). Because of God's abundant lovingkindness, our children and grandchildren have the opportunity to embrace a beautiful heritage too.

In my family and families across the face of this earth, may the Lord raise up generation after generation of worshippers who love and seek Him and proclaim His great name. Amen and amen!

FIVE GENERATIONS

We gathered in our big, sunny kitchen to attempt a family photograph. My grandparents sat on the bench with their older great-great-grandchildren in front and beside them. My mom stood to one side, forming a new row and holding a place for Dad to slip in after he adjusted the tripod and set the camera timer. Brad and I anchored the other side while several children crowded in the middle. Our tall adult sons formed the third row, holding up toddlers and infants so they could be included in the photograph. We jostled and laughed, cajoling wiggly little ones to smile (or at least look toward the camera).

Five generations were included that day—my grandparents, my parents, Brad and me, our twelve children along with the spouses of those who were married, and finally, our grandchildren. Five generations of blessing and legacy and love: evidence of God's graciousness and generosity toward us, and affirmation of a rich, beautiful heritage.

As I look back and see the grace interspersed in my life, I realize that in every season and situation, God was speaking hope and vision over me. Sometimes I immediately recognized His benevolence, while other parts of my story won't reveal their purpose until eternity. But both the joys and hardships have given me a deeper understanding and love of grace—and of Jesus who offers grace upon grace.

I have been able to live my dream. Motherhood was my greatest desire. I believe God gave me that desire, graciously fulfilled it, and then equipped me to walk in it. Serving the next generation is not a glamorous life, but it is a beautiful one—filled with intimacy, influence, and joy. Of course, I faced difficulties and have some regrets, but His faithfulness is woven into every inch of the fabric of my life.

Not everyone gets to live their passion. Some people experience persecution, abuse, trauma, and loss after loss. Their story is no dream come true. Regardless of the particulars of our individual sagas, Jesus continues to invite each of us into a full, abundant life as He graciously draws us to Himself.

No matter what we face in this temporary and broken world, we have an eternal home. One day we will join Jesus there and walk fully in our glorious inheritance. My story, your story, and the story of every believer, for every generation, is always moving toward a glorious fairy-tale-of-them-all ending. We have a future in the magnificence and splendor of heaven, where our faith, at last, will become sight. Jesus, our abundance and true inheritance, will welcome us. And we will all together proclaim this glorious truth:

"Indeed, my heritage is beautiful to me!" (Psalm 16:6).

With Deepest Gratitude

Thank you to my mom and dad, my brother, my husband, and all my sweet children and grandchildren for encouraging me and putting up with the long hours required through the gestation and birth of this dream. I am overwhelmed with the beauty of doing life with you dear ones.

Ann Swindell, it was such a privilege to be a part of your Writing With Grace Mastermind. Your patient teaching and gracious feedback improved my skills immensely. Your gentle encouragement and constant reminder that writing is worship, and that it matters in God's kingdom kept me moving forward when this book felt impossible. Thank you, friend. I can write, because of you.

Katie Williams, in your capable and gracious editor-hands this manuscript became exponentially more cohesive and readable. Thank you for your generosity and insight.

Mom, Kristy Bergthold, Maellen Blodgett, Pat Colloms, Shan Gaither, Deborah Hale, Adelyn Small, and Amanda Turner: Thank you for reading through chapters and giving suggestions while listening to me dream and process for years. Your friendship is precious to me.

Thank you most of all to our gracious God who gives life and gives it abundantly. I praise You for what You have done and for what You will yet do.